Name

Draw a Picture

I Can...

- [ ] use a Capital Letter
  <u>T</u>he cat is big.

- [ ] use spaces

- [ ] sound out words
  d-o-g = dog

- [ ] use a Period .

- [ ] Draw a picture

He is having fun, running under the sun with his new toy gun.

amusement	pistolet	courir	soleil
مرح	مسدس	يركض	شمس

Name: _______________________ Date: _______________________

Today is: [Monday] [Tuesday] [Wednesday]
[Thursday] [Friday]

Direction: Trace and read the sentences.

sac	chiffon	étiquette	remuer
بیگ	چیتھڑا	ٹیگ	واگ

He has many bags.

I see a rag.

I see a tag.

Its tail is wagging.

My Sight Word List

a	in	said
and	is	see
away	it	the
big	jump	three
blue	little	to
can	look	two
come	make	up
down	me	we
find	my	where
for	not	yellow
funny	one	you
go	day	
help	play	
here	red	
I	run	

Name: _______________ Date: _______________

Today is: Monday   Tuesday   Wednesday
          Thursday   Friday

Direction: Trace and read the sentences.

amusement	pistolet	courir	soleil
مرح	بندوف	رن	سورج

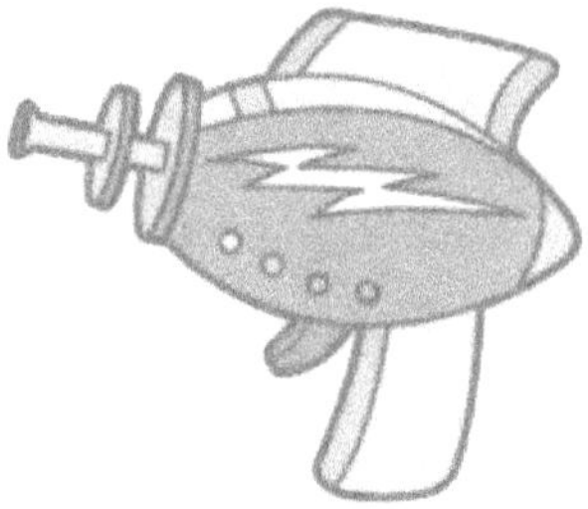

They are having fun.

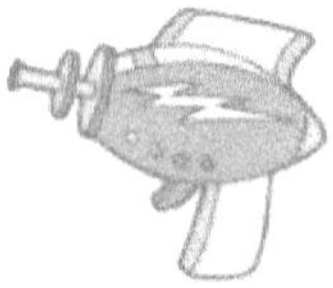

He has a gun.

The bear is running.

The sun is smiling.

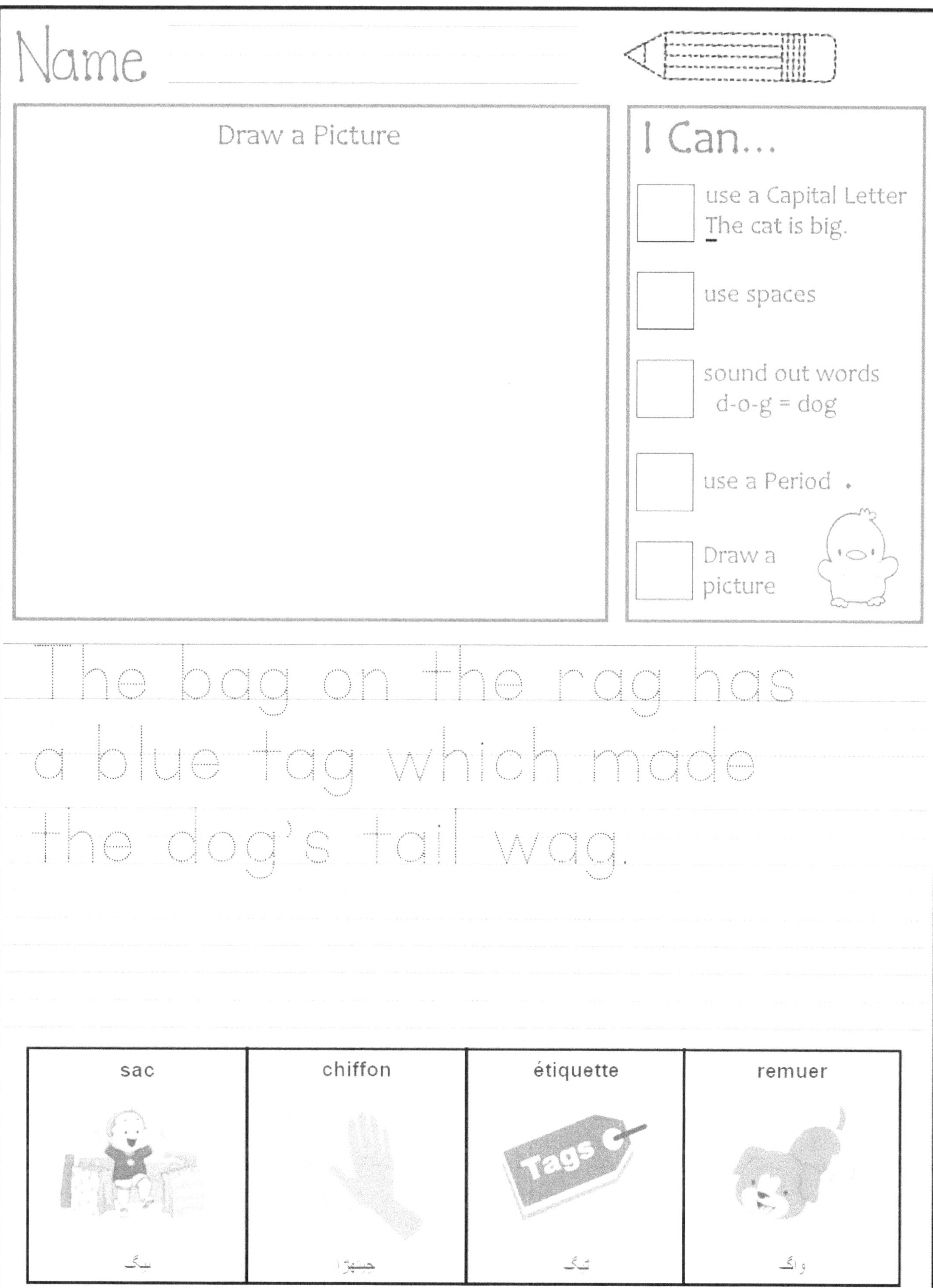

Name

Draw a Picture

I Can...

use a Capital Letter
The cat is big.

use spaces

sound out words
d-o-g = dog

use a Period .

Draw a
picture

The bag on the rag has
a blue tag which made
the dog's tail wag.

sac

chiffon

étiquette

remuer

بیگ

چیزا

تیگ

واگ

Name: ____________________ Date: ____________________

Today is: Monday | Tuesday | Wednesday | Thursday | Friday

Direction: Trace and read the sentences.

canettes	homme	la poêle	van
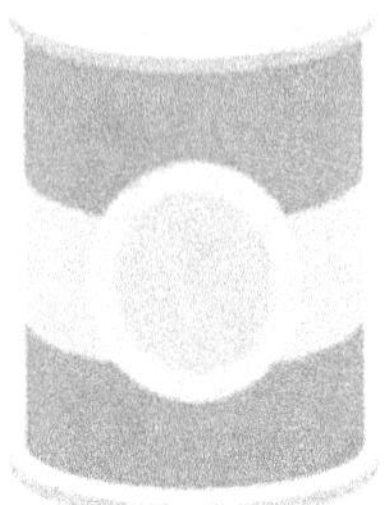			
ایک کین	آدمی	پین	وین

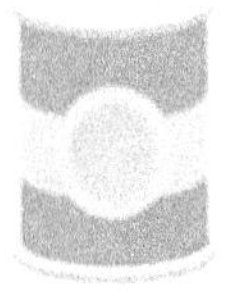

I see a can of soda.

The man is happy.

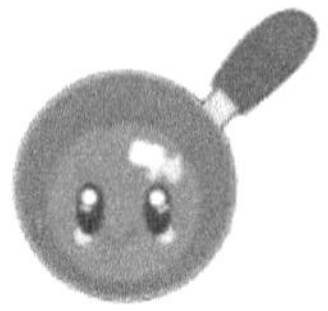

The pan is dirty.

I see a big van.

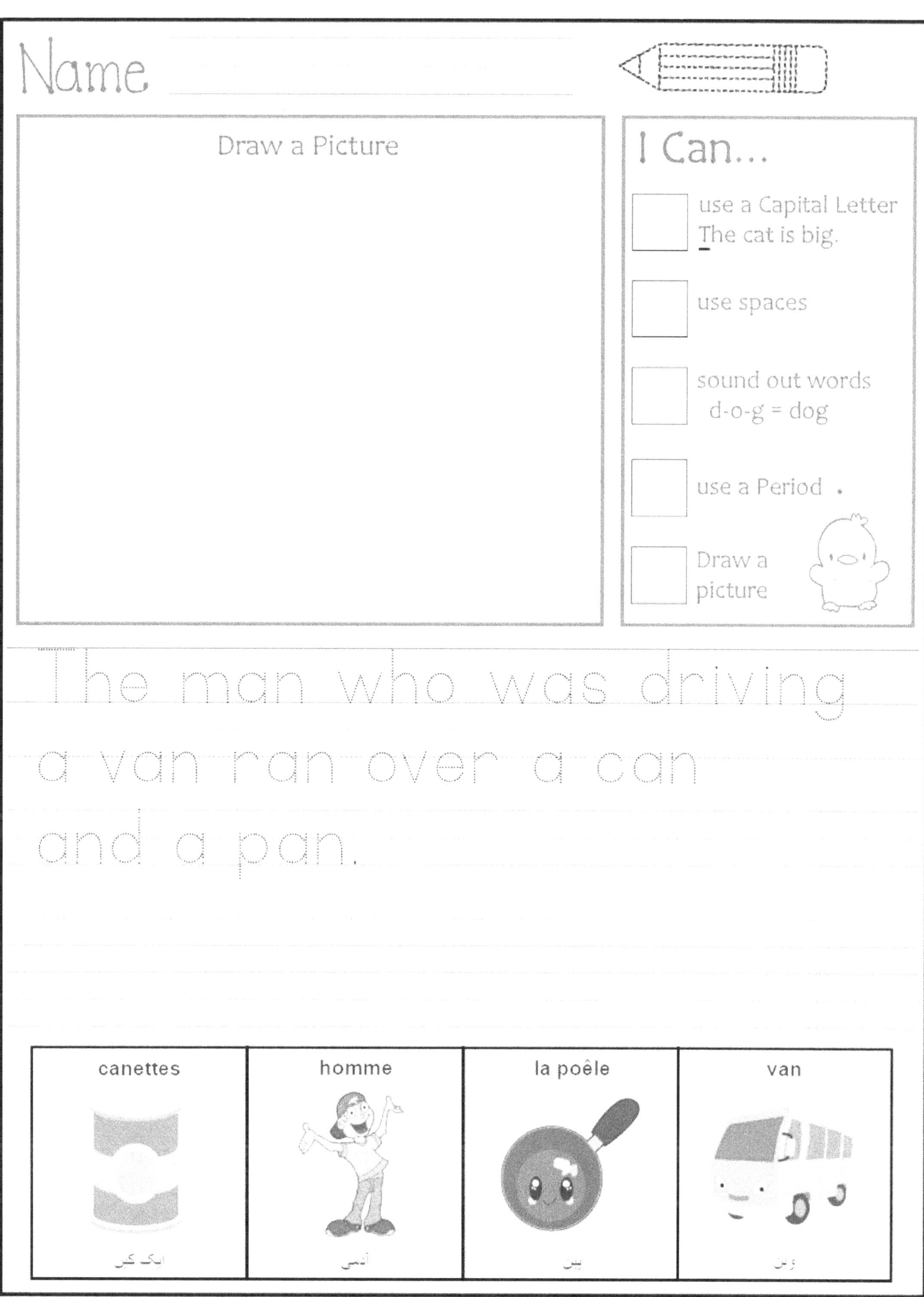

Name

Draw a Picture

I Can...

use a Capital Letter
The cat is big.

use spaces

sound out words
d-o-g = dog

use a Period .

Draw a
picture

The man who was driving
a van ran over a can
and a pan.

canettes

homme

la poêle

van

Name: _______________ Date: _______________

Today is: | Monday | Tuesday | Wednesday |
| Thursday | Friday |

Direction: Trace and read the sentences.

| couper | intestin | cabane | écrou |

He cut his nails.

He has a gut.

This is a small hut.

It is holding a nut.

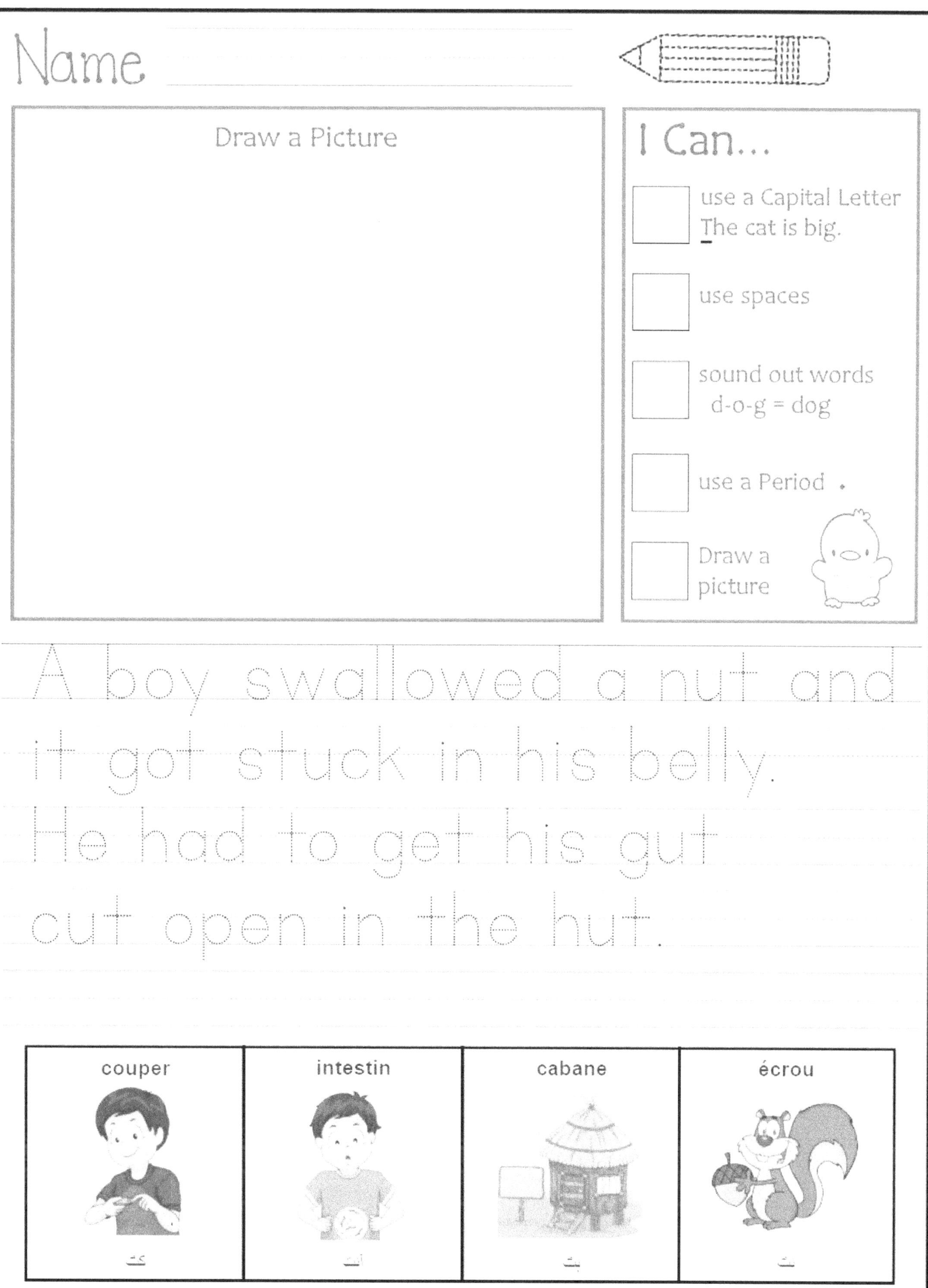

Name

Draw a Picture

I Can...

use a Capital Letter
The cat is big.

use spaces

sound out words
d-o-g = dog

use a Period .

Draw a
picture

A boy swallowed a nut and
it got stuck in his belly.
He had to get his gut
cut open in the hut.

couper

intestin

cabane

écrou

Name: _________________ Date: _____________

Today is: | Monday | Tuesday | Wednesday |
| Thursday | Friday |

Direction: Trace and read the sentences.

graisse	chat	chapeau	tapis
جرى	كت	توبى	جالى

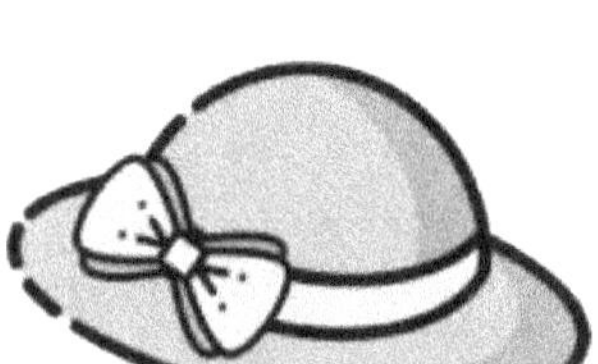

I see a fat dog.

This is my little cat.

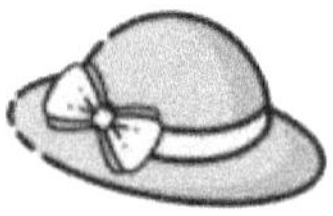

I like this hat.

I see a big mat.

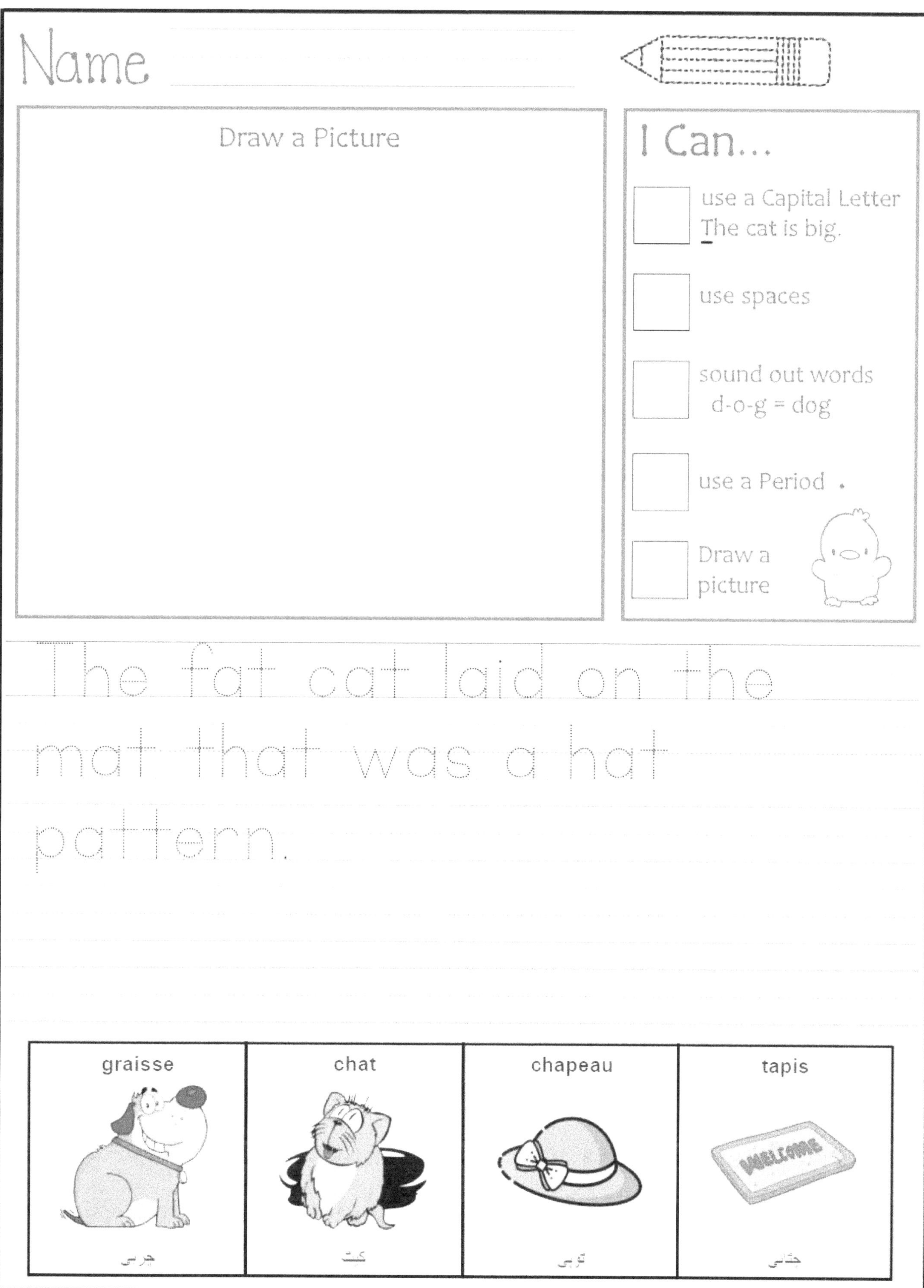

Name

Draw a Picture

I Can...

use a Capital Letter
The cat is big.

use spaces

sound out words
d-o-g = dog

use a Period .

Draw a
picture

The fat cat laid on the mat that was a hat pattern.

graisse

chat

chapeau

tapis

Name: _______________ Date: _______________

Today is: Monday   Tuesday   Wednesday
           Thursday   Friday

Direction: Trace and read the sentences.

taxi	laboratoire	languette	crabe

The cab is fast.

The lab is exciting.

The tab is long.

We found a crab.

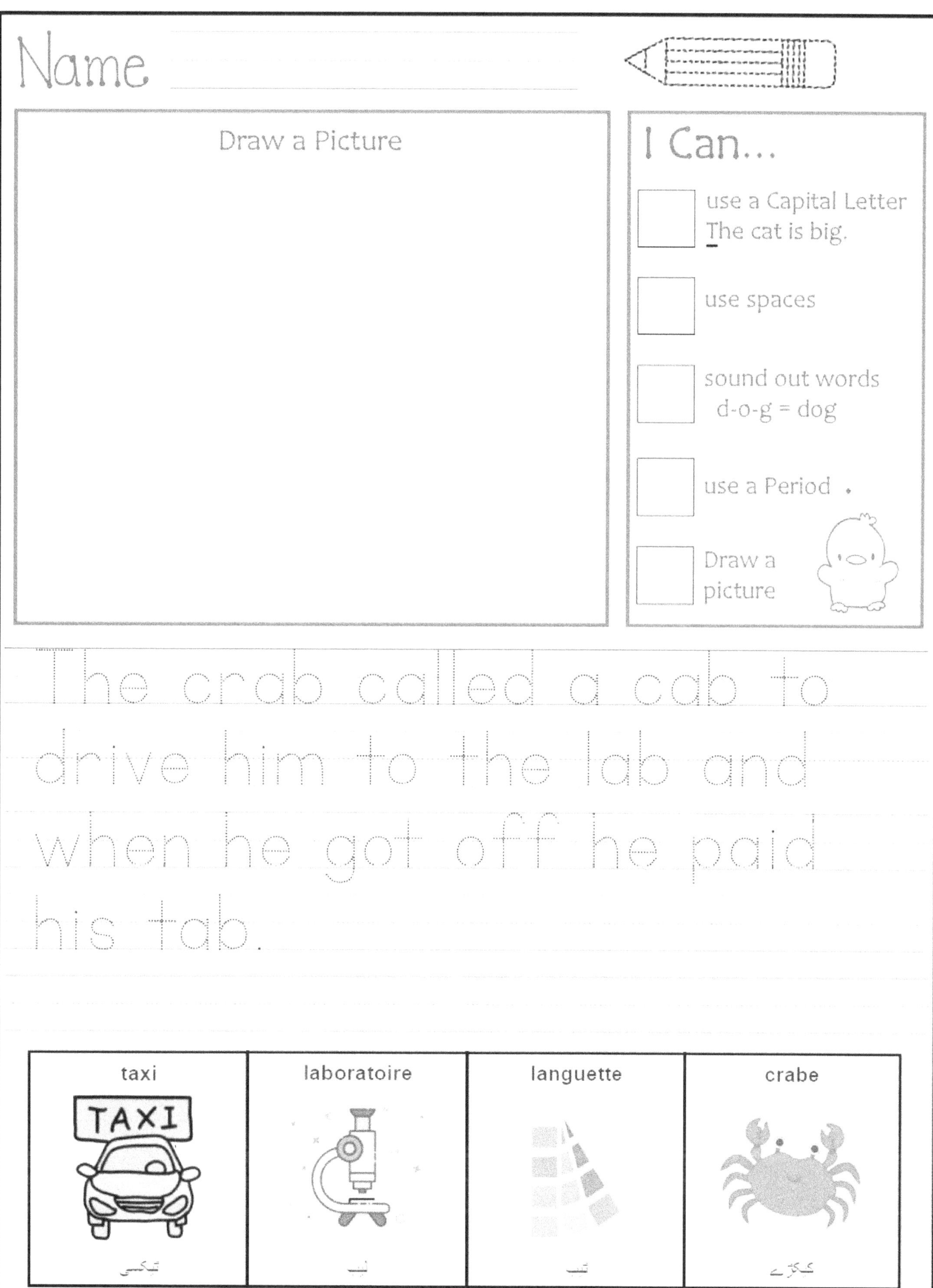

Name

Draw a Picture

I Can...

use a Capital Letter
The cat is big.

use spaces

sound out words
d-o-g = dog

use a Period .

Draw a
picture

The crab called a cab to
drive him to the lab and
when he got off he paid
his tab.

taxi

laboratoire

languette

crabe

Name: _______________ Date: _______________

Today is: | Monday | Tuesday | Wednesday |
| Thursday | Friday |

Direction: Trace and read the sentences.

jambon	confiture	mouton	palourde
بام	حدم	بيىز	ئئل

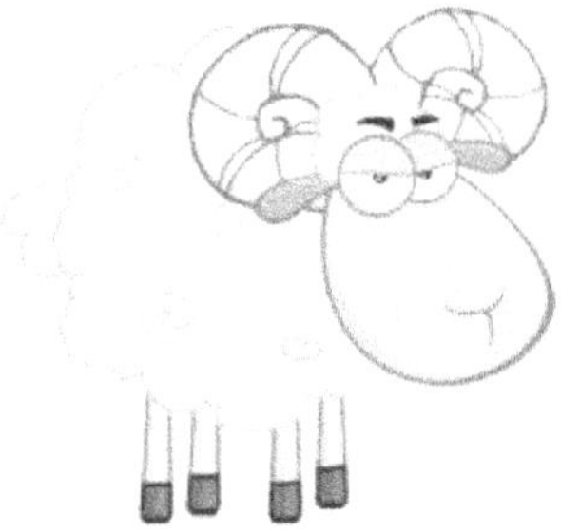

I like to eat ham.

We like to eat jam.

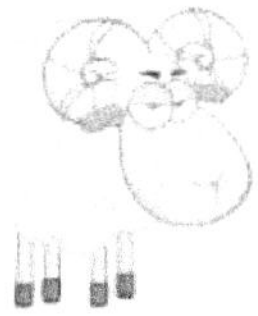

The ram is big.

The clam is pretty.

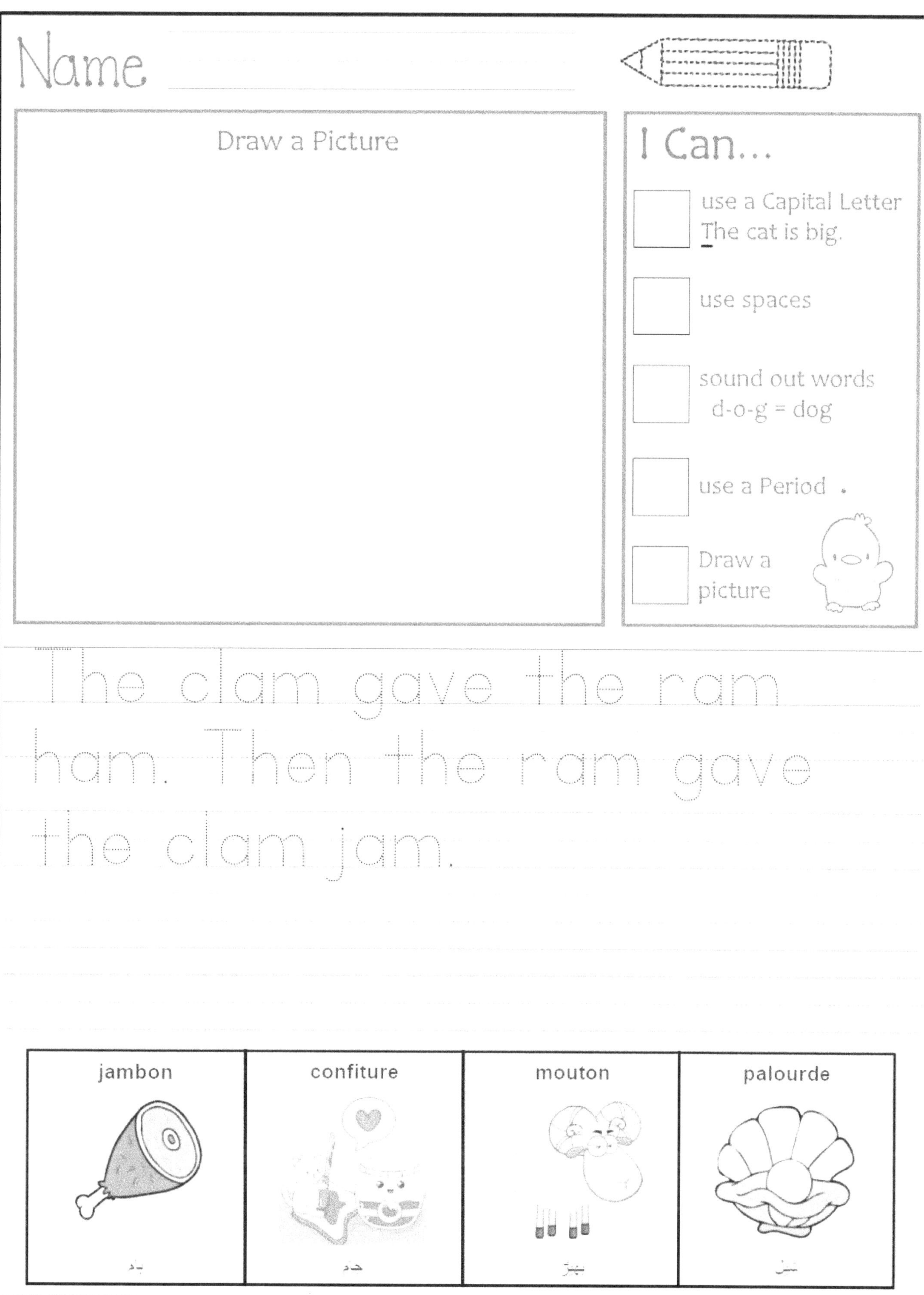

Name

Draw a Picture

I Can...

use a Capital Letter
The cat is big.

use spaces

sound out words
d-o-g = dog

use a Period .

Draw a
picture

The clam gave the ram
ham. Then the ram gave
the clam jam.

jambon

confiture

mouton

palourde

Name: ______________________ Date: ______________________

Today is: Monday | Tuesday | Wednesday | Thursday | Friday

Direction: Trace and read the sentences.

lit	de premier plan	rouge	mariage
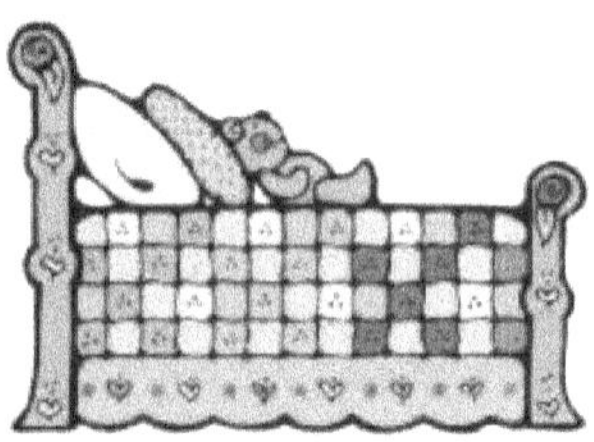			
بستر	معروف	سرخ	شادی

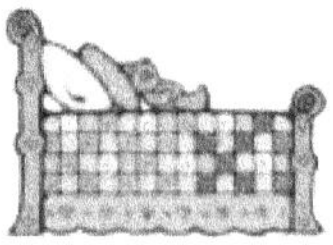 This is my little bed.

 He led us to safety.

 The apple is red.

 He asks her to wed.

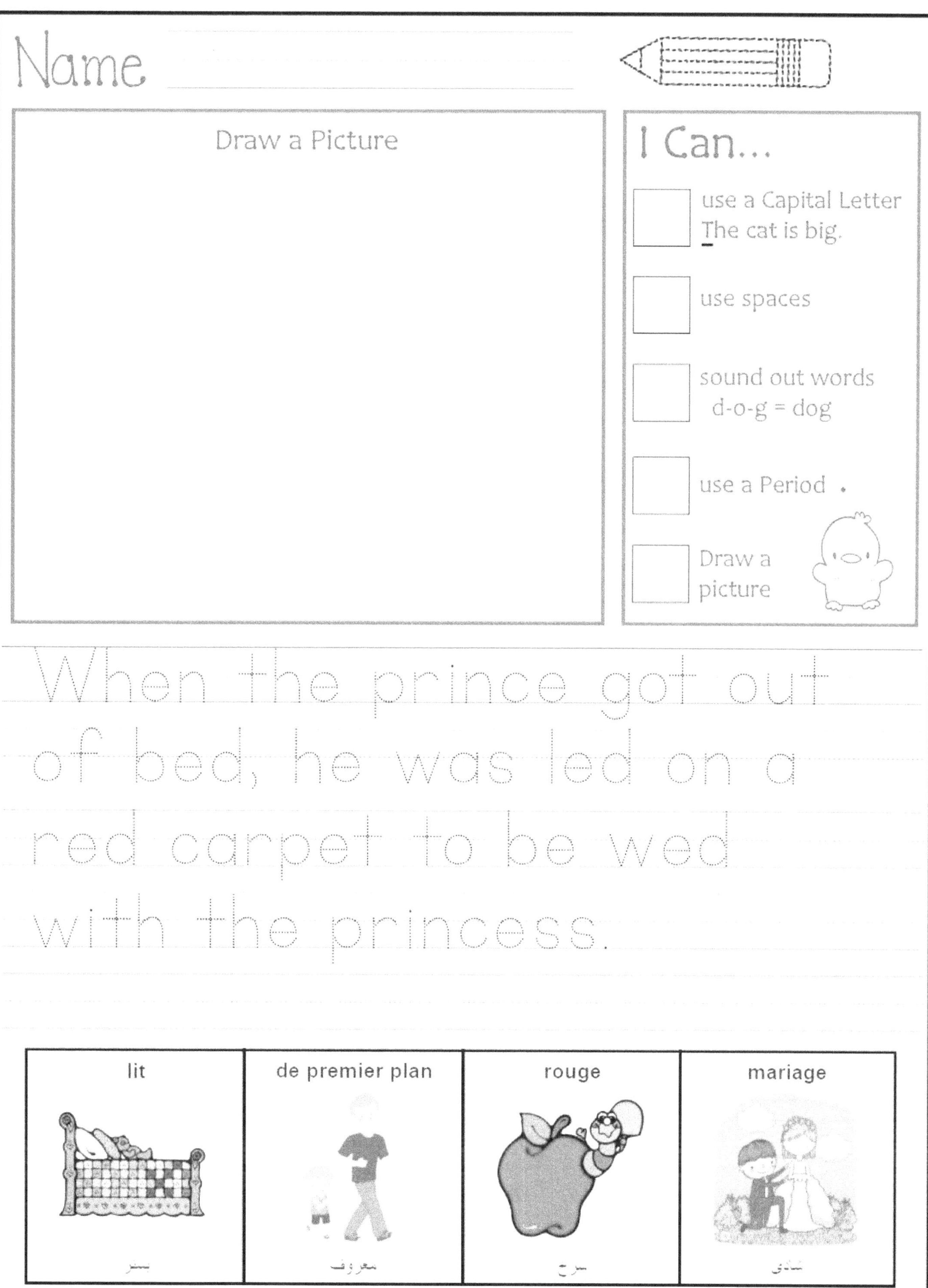
Name

Draw a Picture

I Can...

use a Capital Letter
The cat is big.

use spaces

sound out words
d-o-g = dog

use a Period .

Draw a
picture

When the prince got out
of bed, he was led on a
red carpet to be wed
with the princess.

lit

de premier plan

rouge

mariage

Today is: Monday Tuesday Wednesday Thursday Friday

Direction: Trace and read the sentences.

mauvais	papa	furieux	triste
برا	والد	پاگل	اداس

This apple is bad.

My dad is very kind.

The reindeer is mad.

The little cat is sad.

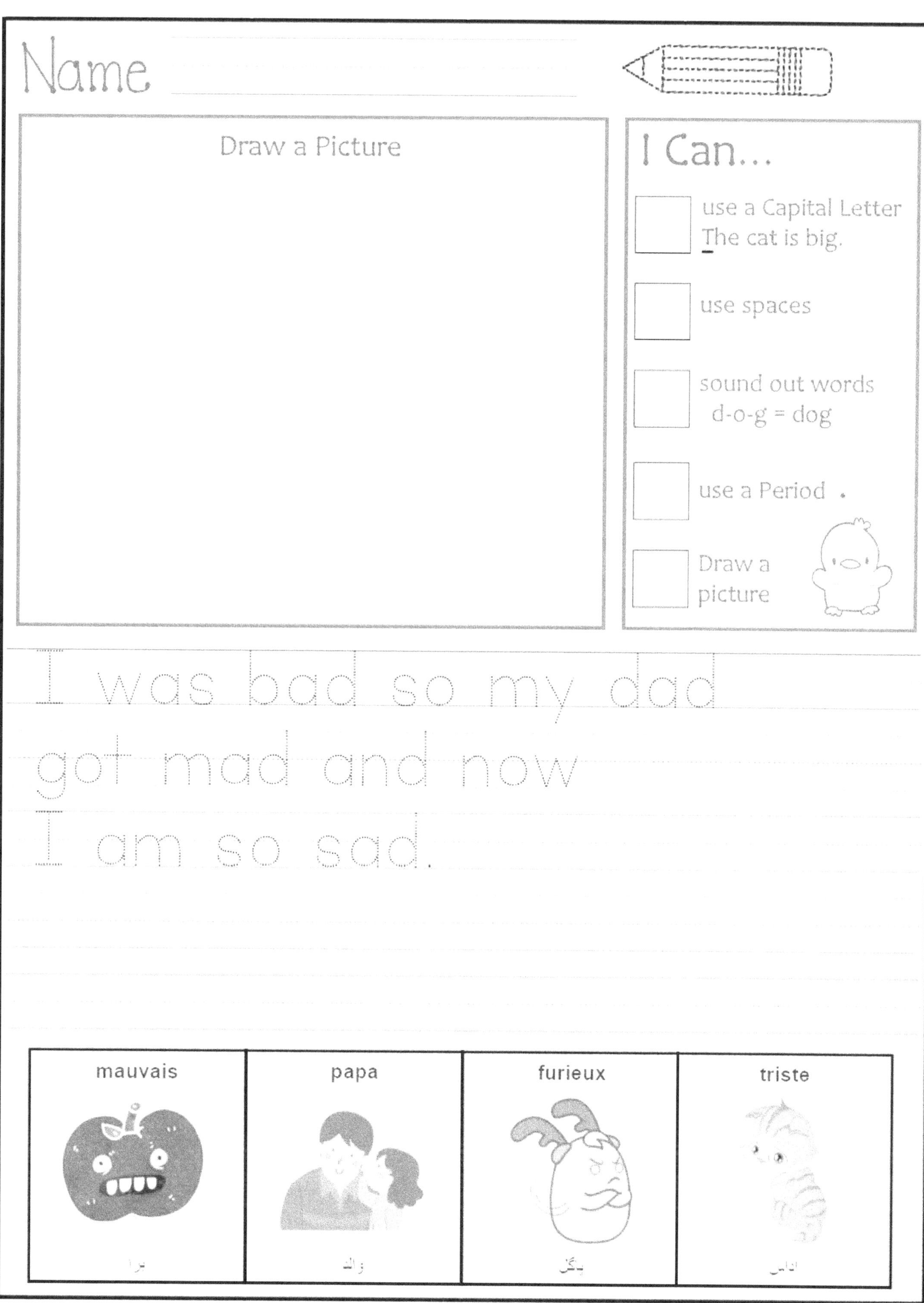

Name
Draw a Picture
I Can...
use a Capital Letter
The cat is big.
use spaces
sound out words
d-o-g = dog
use a Period .
Draw a picture
I was bad so my dad got mad and now I am so sad.
mauvais
papa
furieux
triste

Name: _______________________ Date: _______________

Today is: | Monday | Tuesday | Wednesday |
| Thursday | Friday |

Direction: Trace and read the sentences.

| animal den | poule | écuries | dix |
| ماند | مرغي | اصطبل | نس |

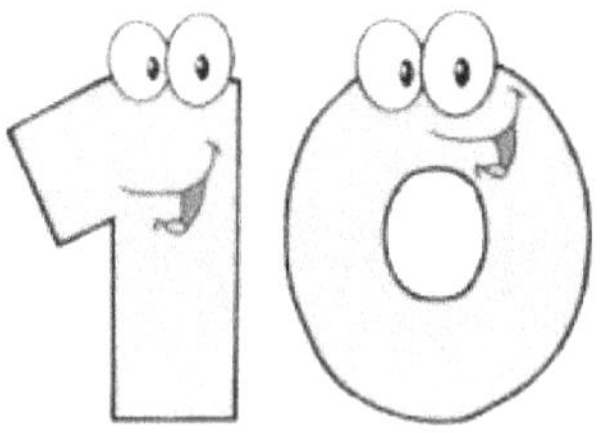

It is a den.

The hens lay eggs.

She has a good pen.

The ten is smiling.

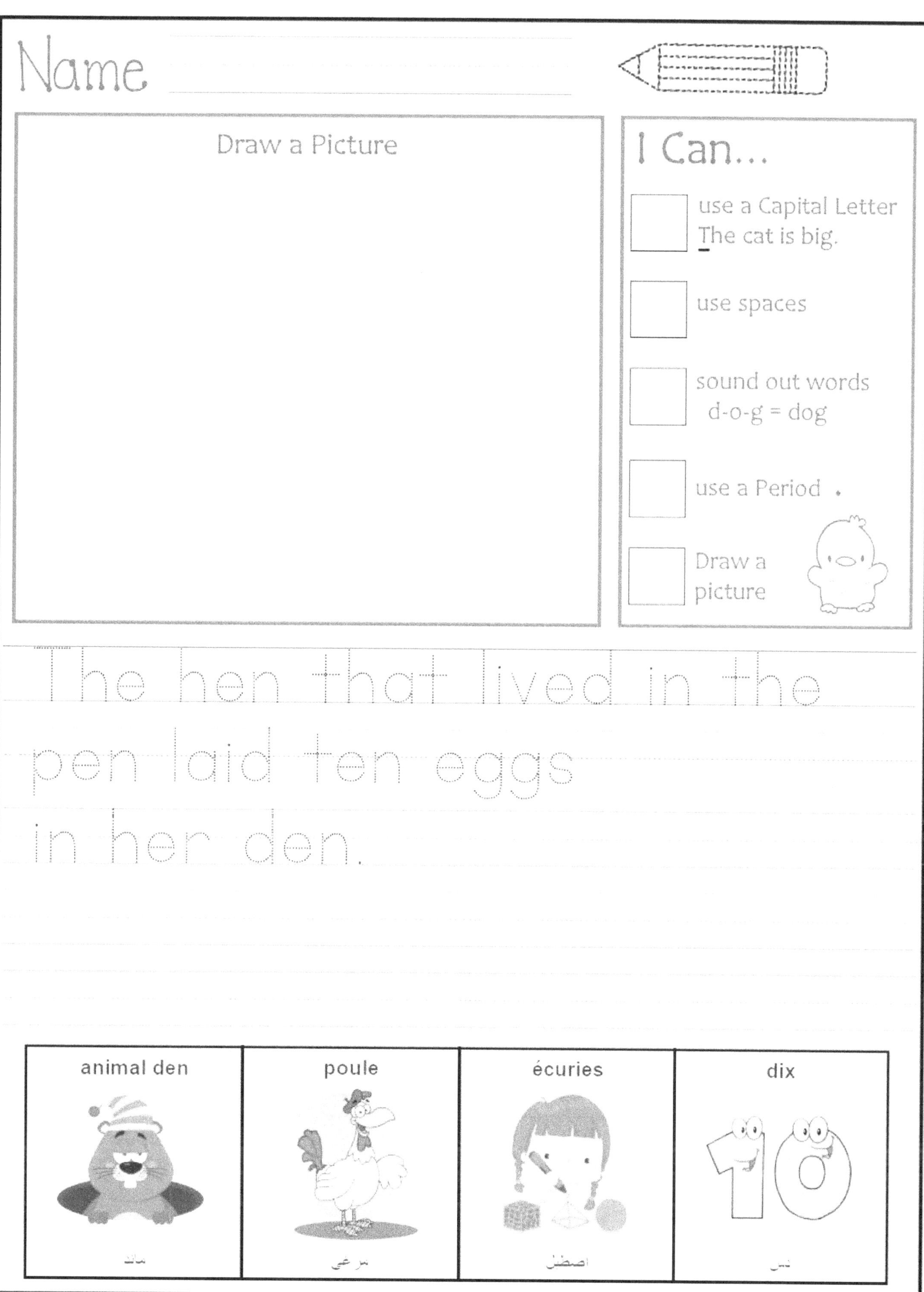

Name
Draw a Picture
I Can...
use a Capital Letter
The cat is big.
use spaces
sound out words
d-o-g = dog
use a Period .
Draw a
picture
The hen that lived in the
pen laid ten eggs
in her den.
animal den
poule
écuries
dix

Name: _______________ Date: _______________

Today is: | Monday | Tuesday | Wednesday |
| Thursday | Friday |

Direction: Trace and read the sentences.

| gommeux | maman | somme | tambour |

I like to chew gum.

My mum is kind!

I can do a sum!

The drum is big.

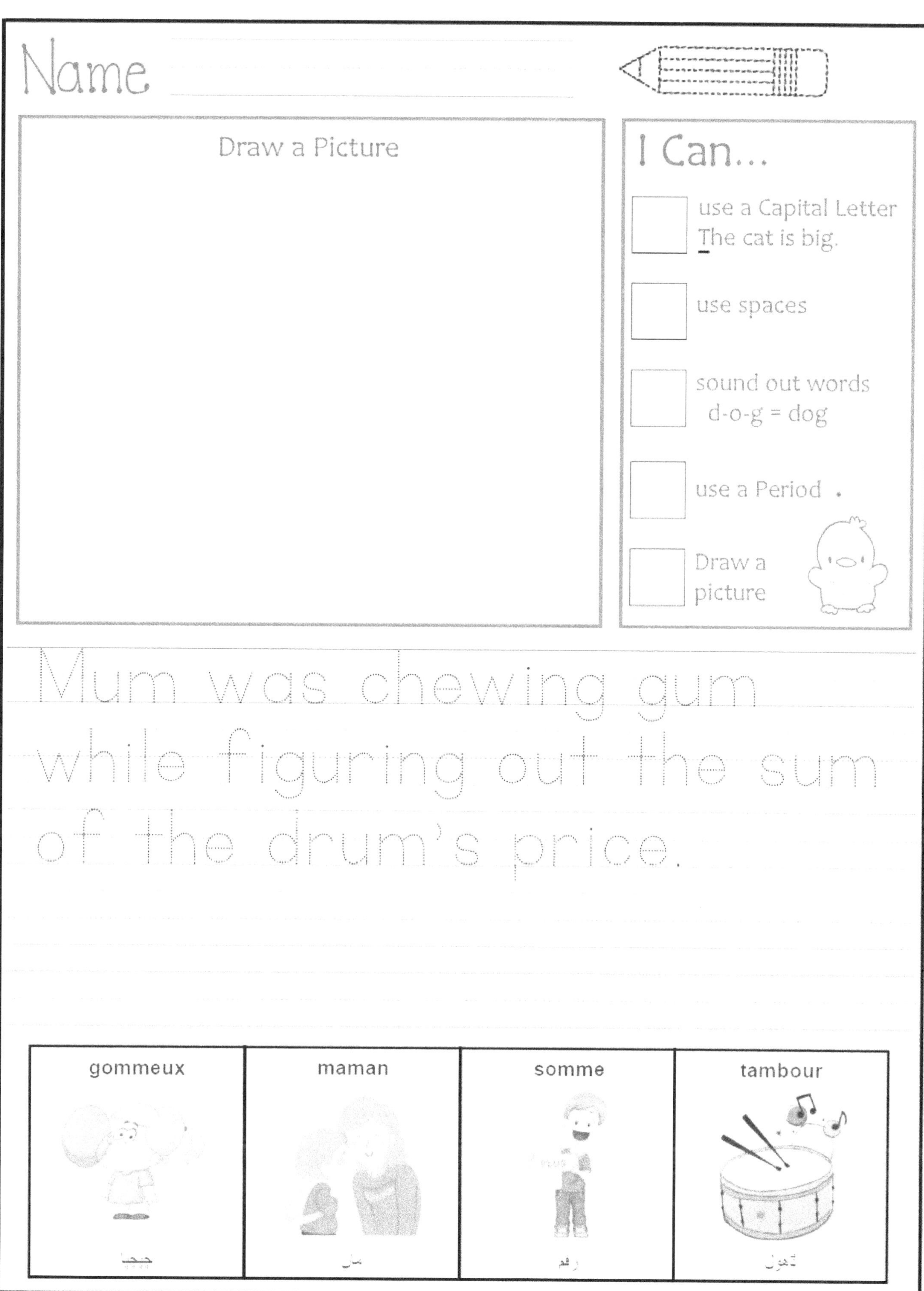

Name
Draw a Picture
I Can...
use a Capital Letter
The cat is big.
use spaces
sound out words
d-o-g = dog
use a Period .
Draw a picture
Mum was chewing gum while figuring out the sum of the drum's price.
gommeux
maman
somme
tambour

Name: _______________ Date: _______________

Today is: | Monday | Tuesday | Wednesday |
| Thursday | Friday |

Direction: Trace and read the sentences.

| offre | cacher | enfant | couvercle |
| بولی | چھپائش | بچہ | ڈھکن |

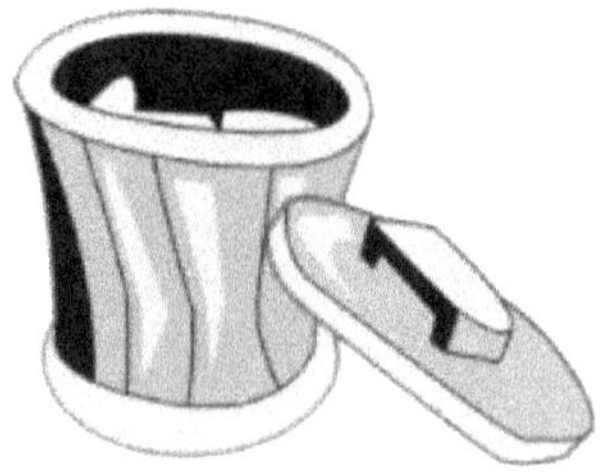

He likes to bid.

He is hiding.

The kid like to play.

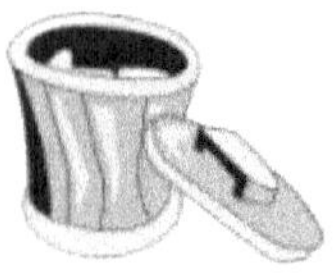

I see a lid.

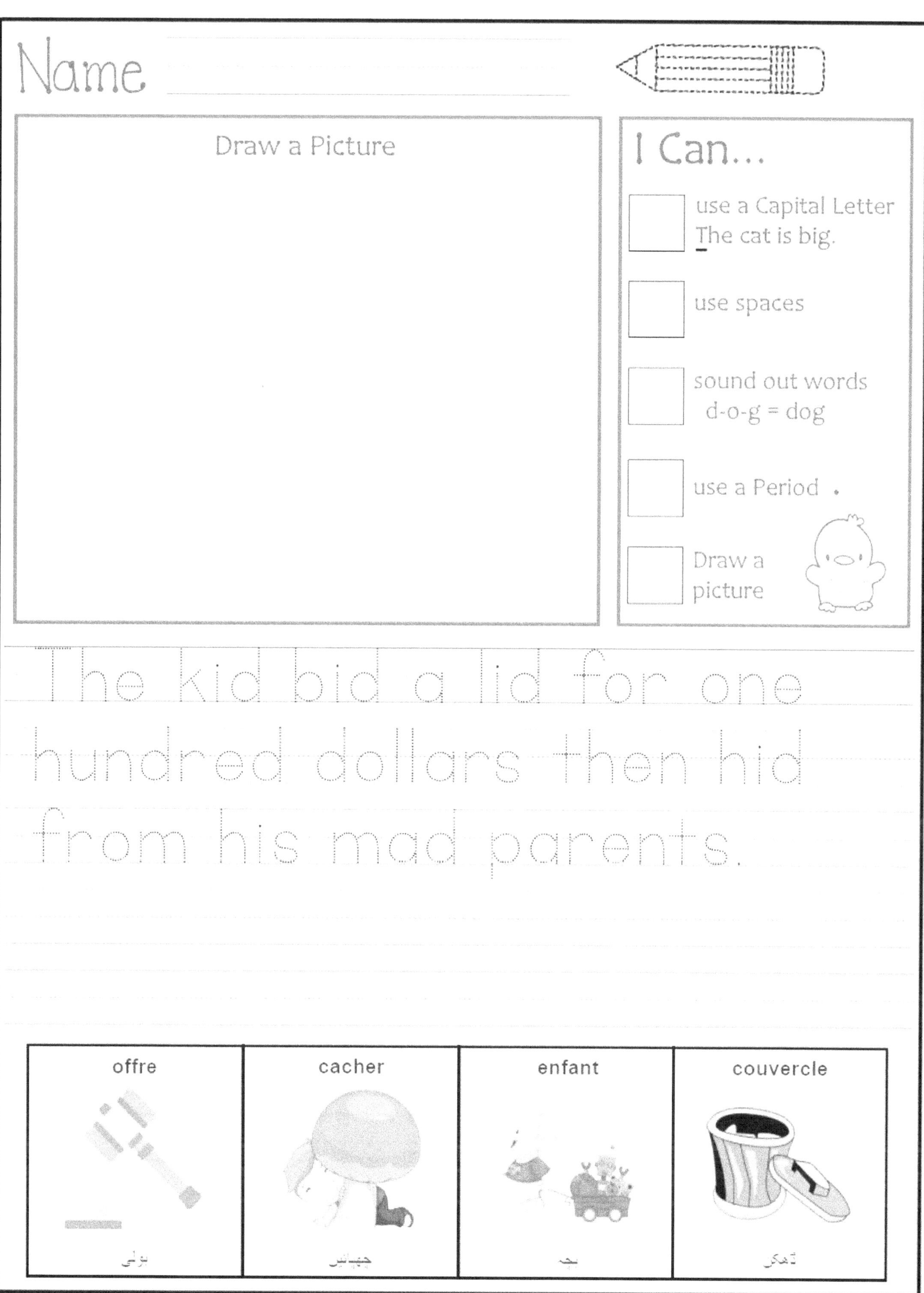

Name _______________

Draw a Picture

I Can...

- [ ] use a Capital Letter
  The cat is big.
- [ ] use spaces
- [ ] sound out words
  d-o-g = dog
- [ ] use a Period .
- [ ] Draw a picture

The kid bid a lid for one hundred dollars then hid from his mad parents.

offre	cacher	enfant	couvercle

Name: ____________________ Date: ____________________

Today is: Monday | Tuesday | Wednesday | Thursday | Friday

Direction: Trace and read the sentences.

gros	creuser	porc	perruque
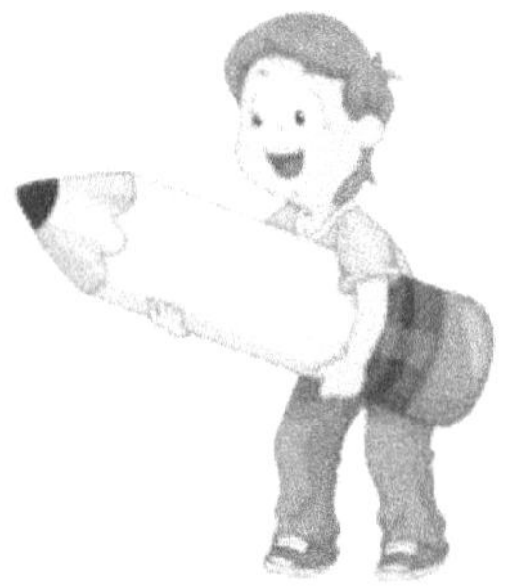	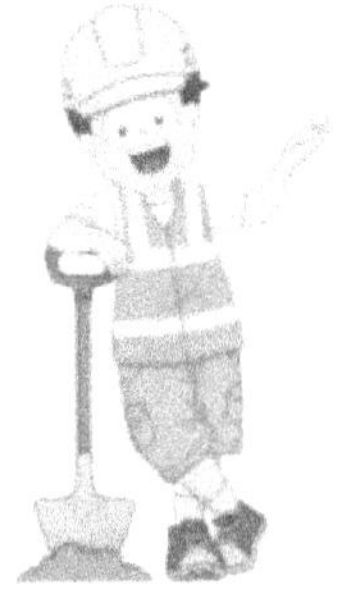	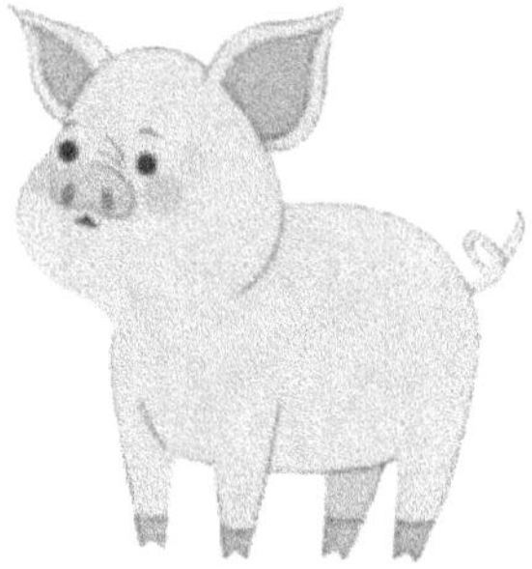	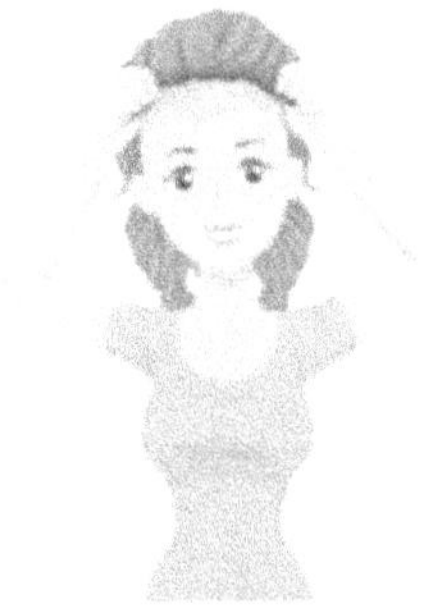
بڑا	کھودنا	سور	وگ

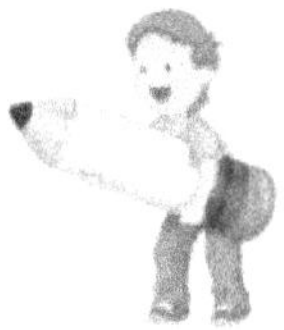 That is a big pencil.

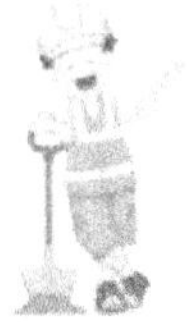 He will dig up a hole.

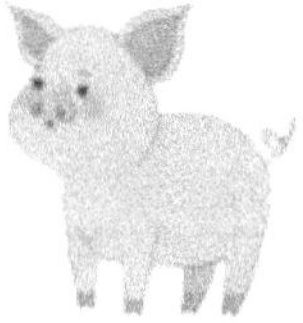 The pig is fat.

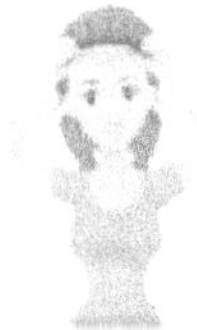 She puts on a wig.

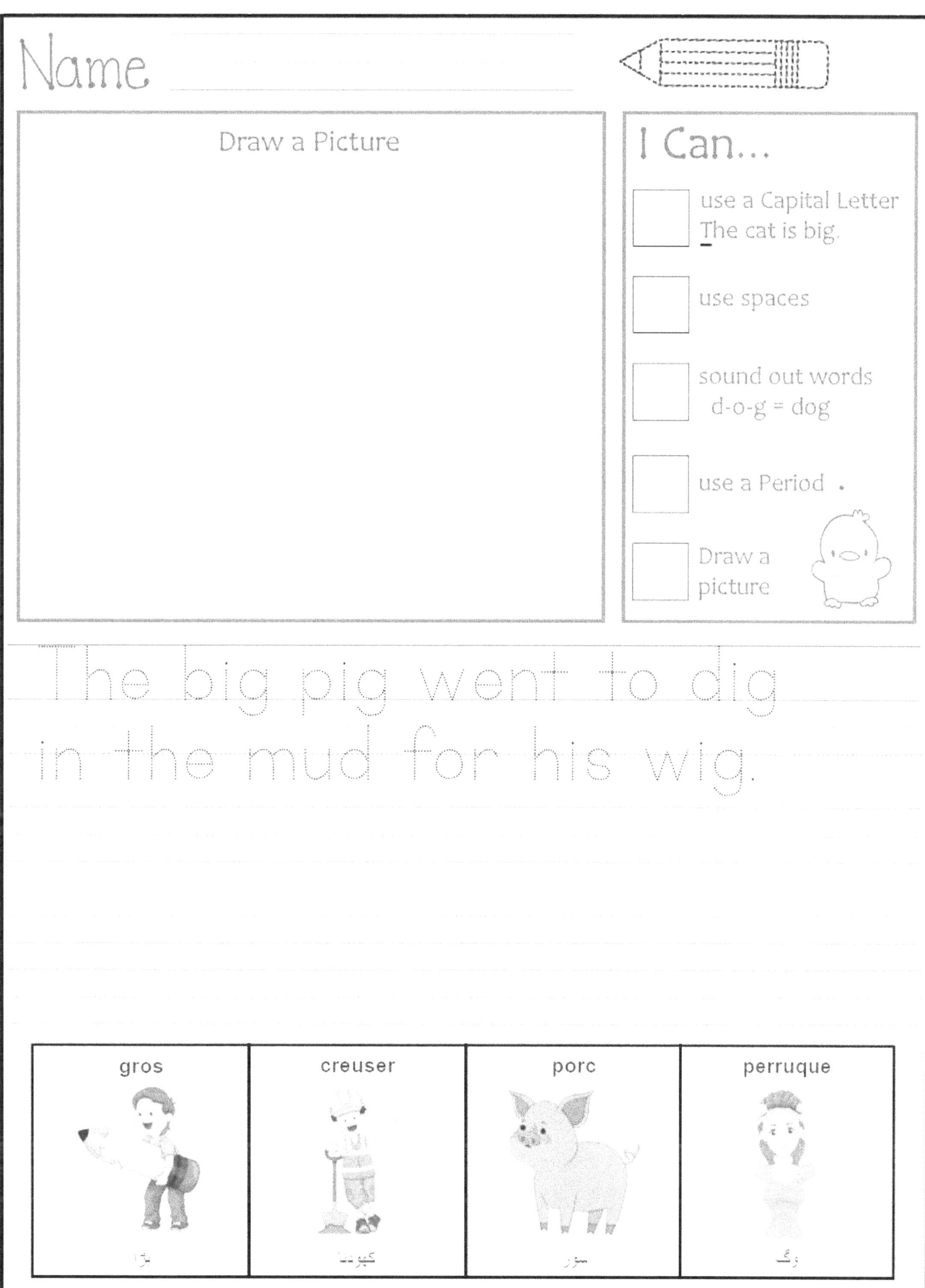

Name

Draw a Picture

I Can...

use a Capital Letter
The cat is big.

use spaces

sound out words
d-o-g = dog

use a Period .

Draw a
picture

The big pig went to dig
in the mud for his wig.

gros

creuser

porc

perruque

Name: __________________ Date: __________

Today is: [Monday] [Tuesday] [Wednesday]
[Thursday] [Friday]

Direction: Trace and read the sentences.

poubelle 	ailette 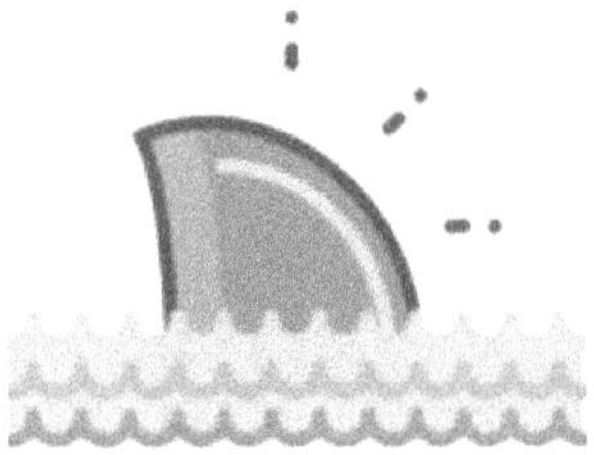	épingle 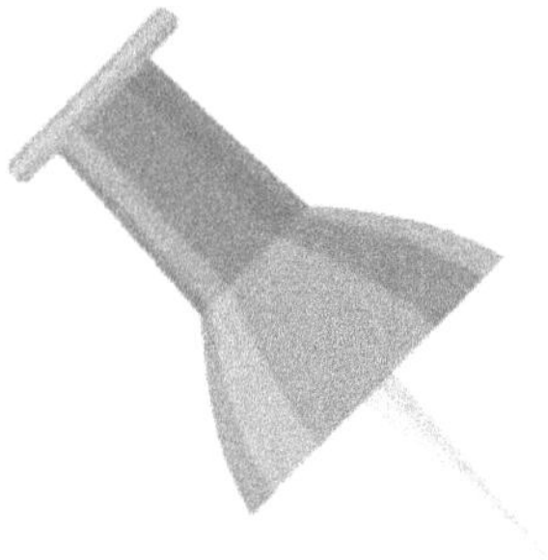	gagner 

ایک ٹوکری
فن
پن
جیت

It is a recycle bin.

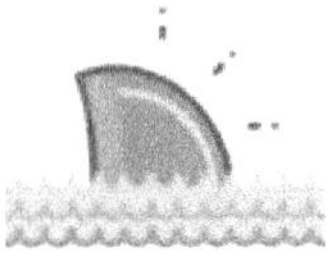

The shark has a fin.

The pin is pointy.

He won the match.

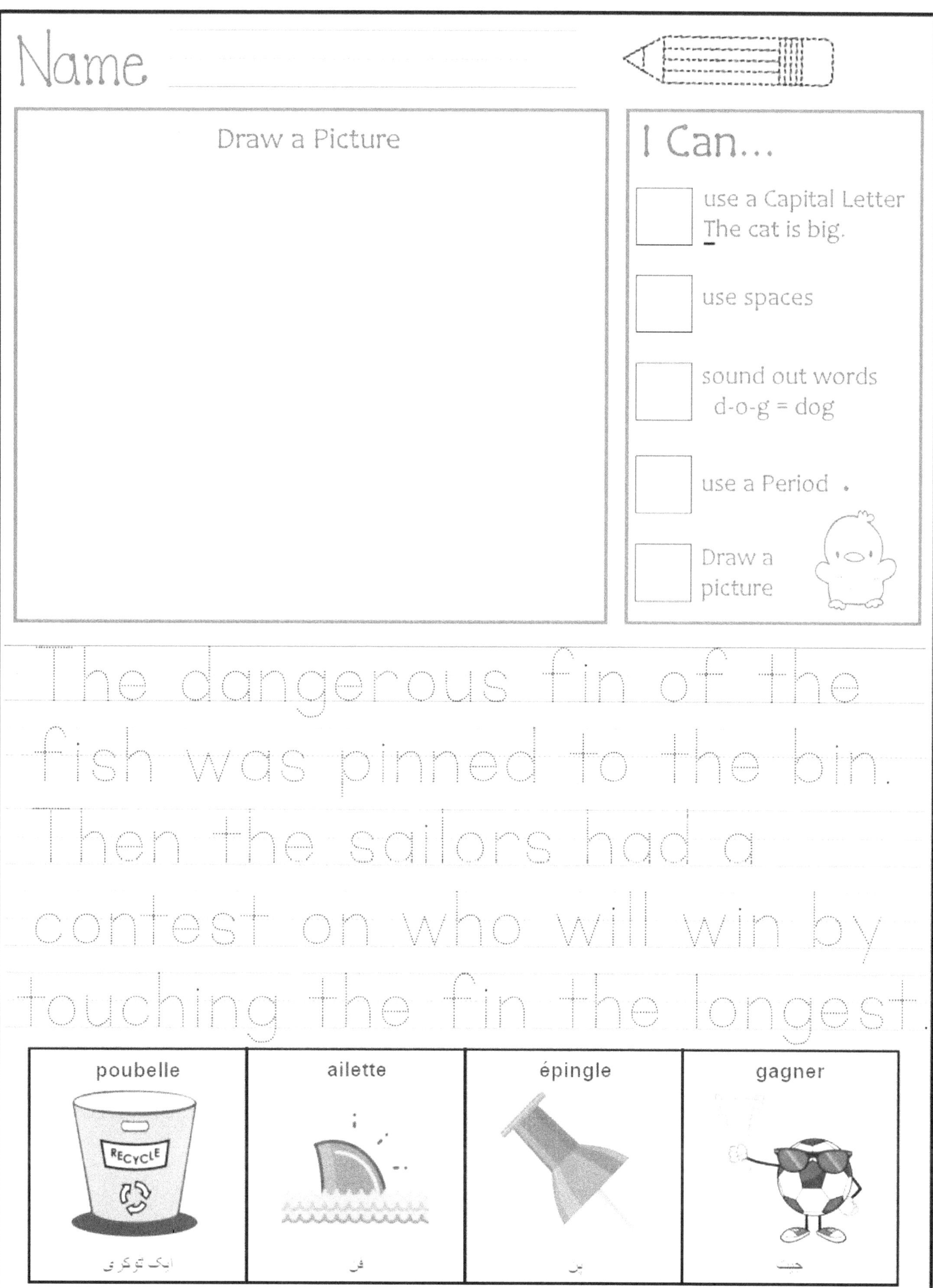

Name

Draw a Picture

I Can...

use a Capital Letter
The cat is big.

use spaces

sound out words
d-o-g = dog

use a Period .

Draw a
picture

The dangerous fin of the
fish was pinned to the bin.
Then the sailors had a
contest on who will win by
touching the fin the longest.

poubelle
RECYCLE
ایک ٹوکری

ailette
ف

épingle
پ

gagner
ج

Name: ______________________ Date: ______________________

Today is: Monday | Tuesday | Wednesday | Thursday | Friday

Direction: Trace and read the sentences.

hanche	lèvres	pincer	boisson
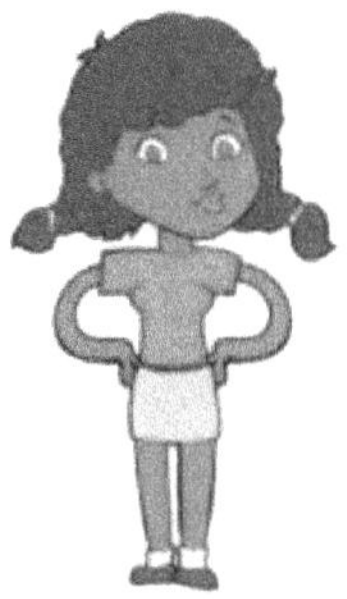	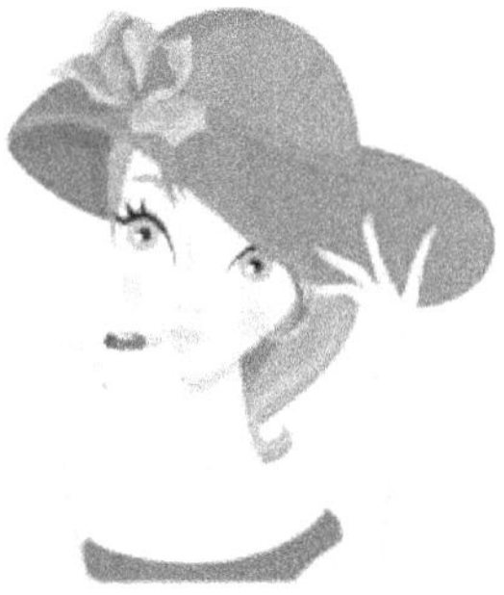	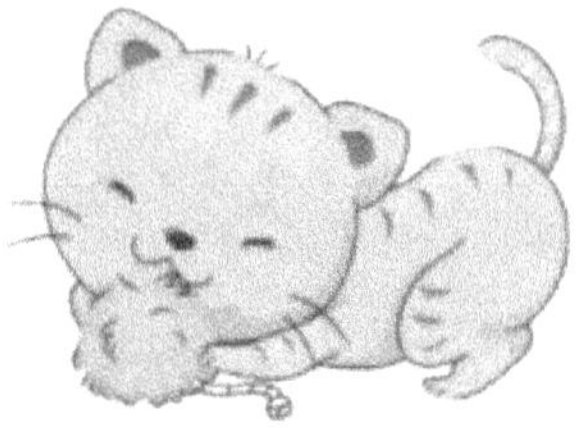	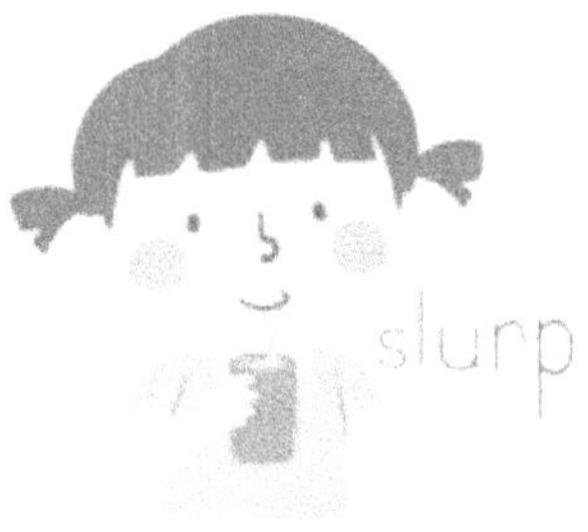
بيب	بونك	نيب	يبو

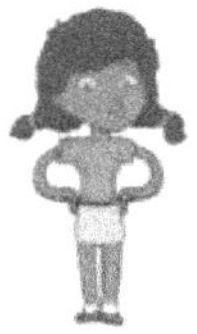

This is my hip.

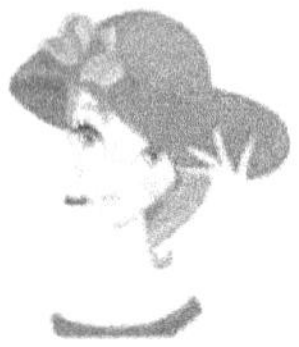

Her lips are red.

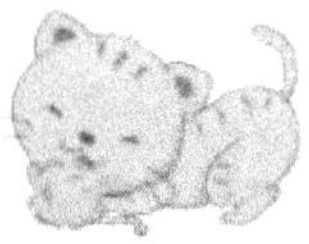

It is nipping its toy.

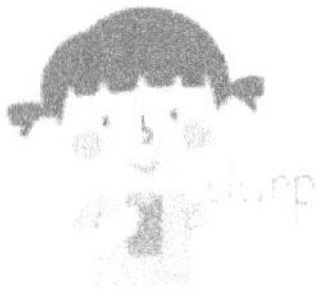

She is sipping.

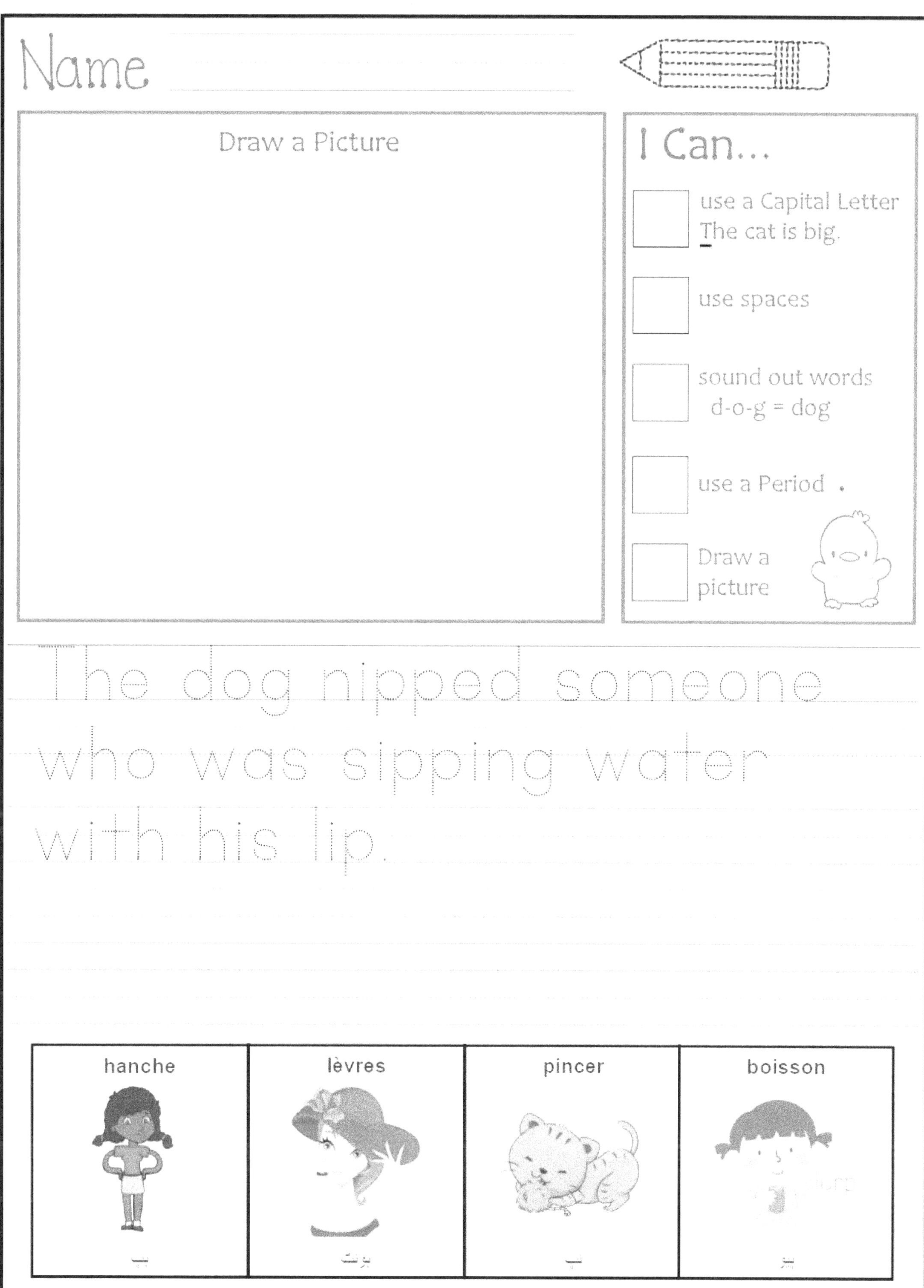

Name

Draw a Picture

I Can...

use a Capital Letter
The cat is big.

use spaces

sound out words
d-o-g = dog

use a Period .

Draw a
picture

The dog nipped someone
who was sipping water
with his lip.

hanche
lèvres
pincer
boisson

Name: ____________________ Date: ____________________

Today is: Monday Tuesday Wednesday Thursday Friday

Direction: Trace and read the sentences.

en forme	frappé	trousse	asseoir
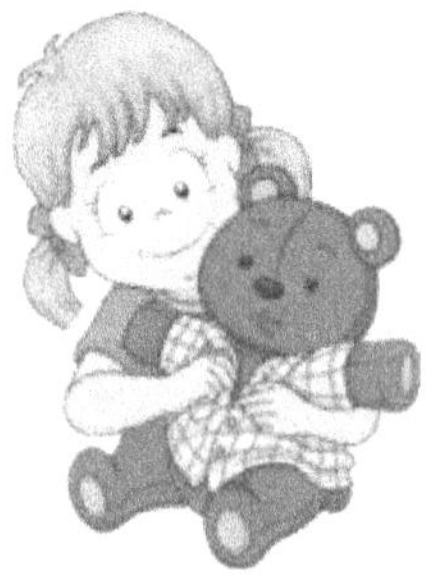	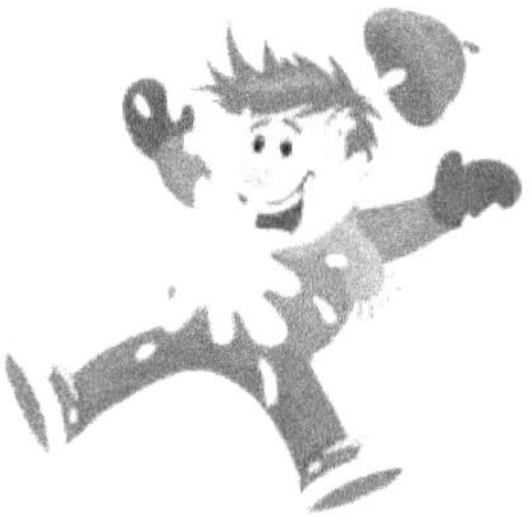	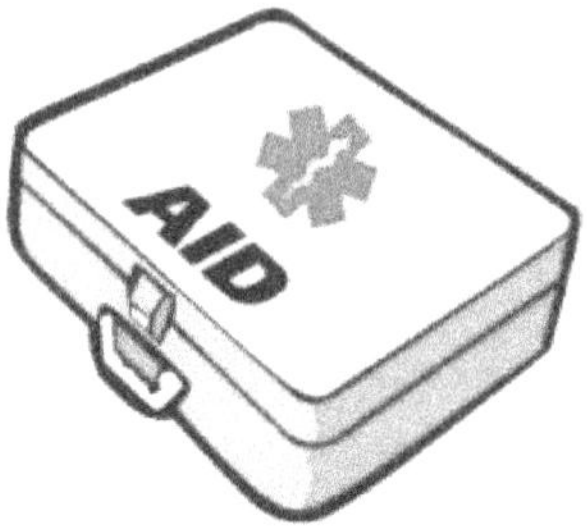	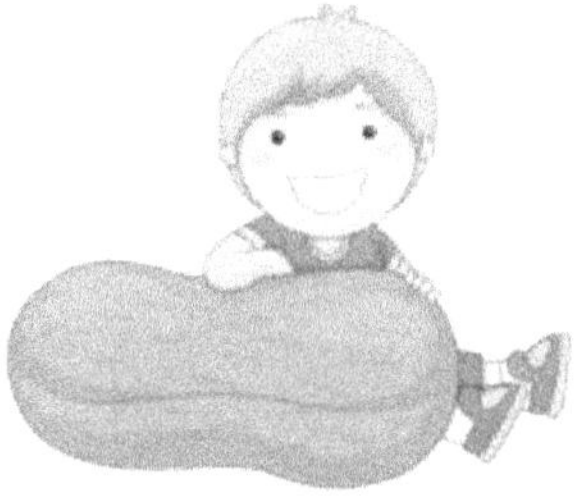
فٹ	مارا	کٹ	بیٹھ

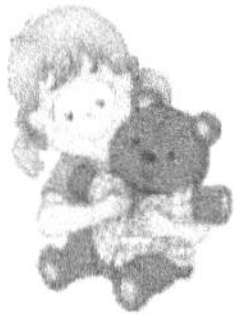

It is perfectly fit.

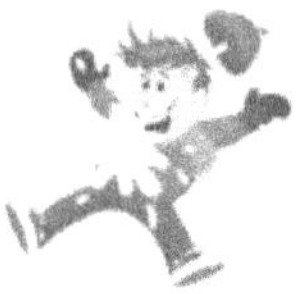

They hit each other.

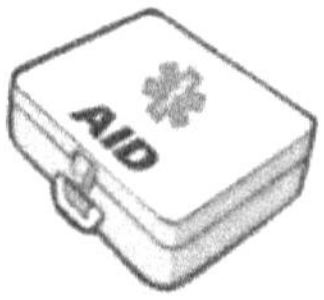

That is a safety kit.

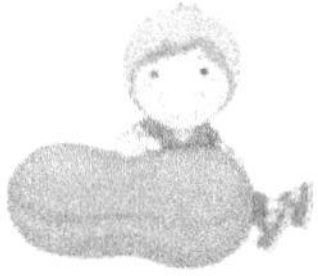

He is sitting.

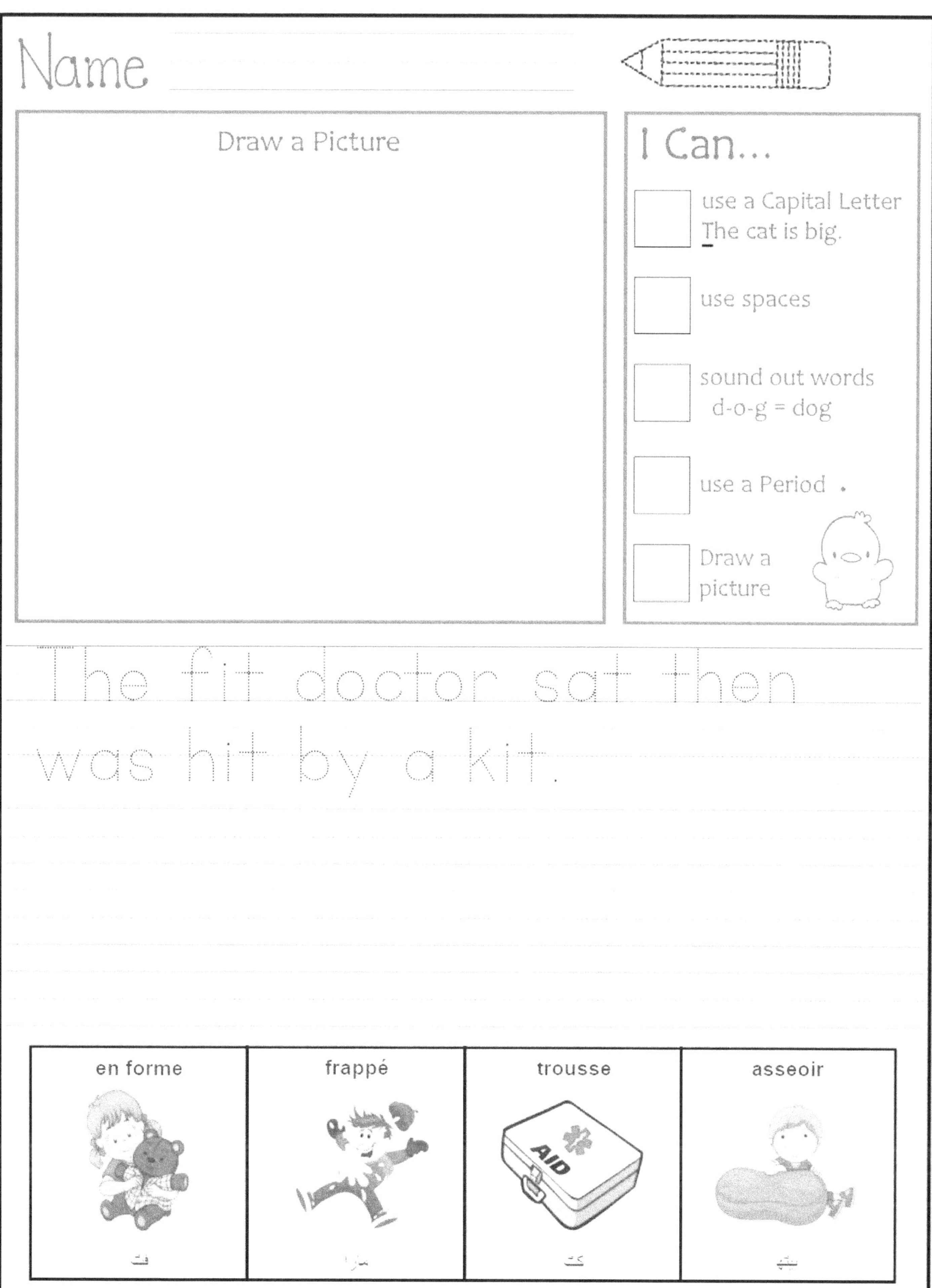

Name
Draw a Picture
I Can...
use a Capital Letter
The cat is big.
use spaces
sound out words
d-o-g = dog
use a Period .
Draw a picture
The fit doctor sat then was hit by a kit.
en forme
frappé
trousse
asseoir

Name: ____________________ Date: ____________________

Today is: Monday | Tuesday | Wednesday | Thursday | Friday

Direction: Trace and read the sentences.

blé	emploi	rob	pleurer

مکئی	نوکری	چوری	رونا

I ate corn on the cob.

This is my job.

He is robbing.

The girl is sobbing.

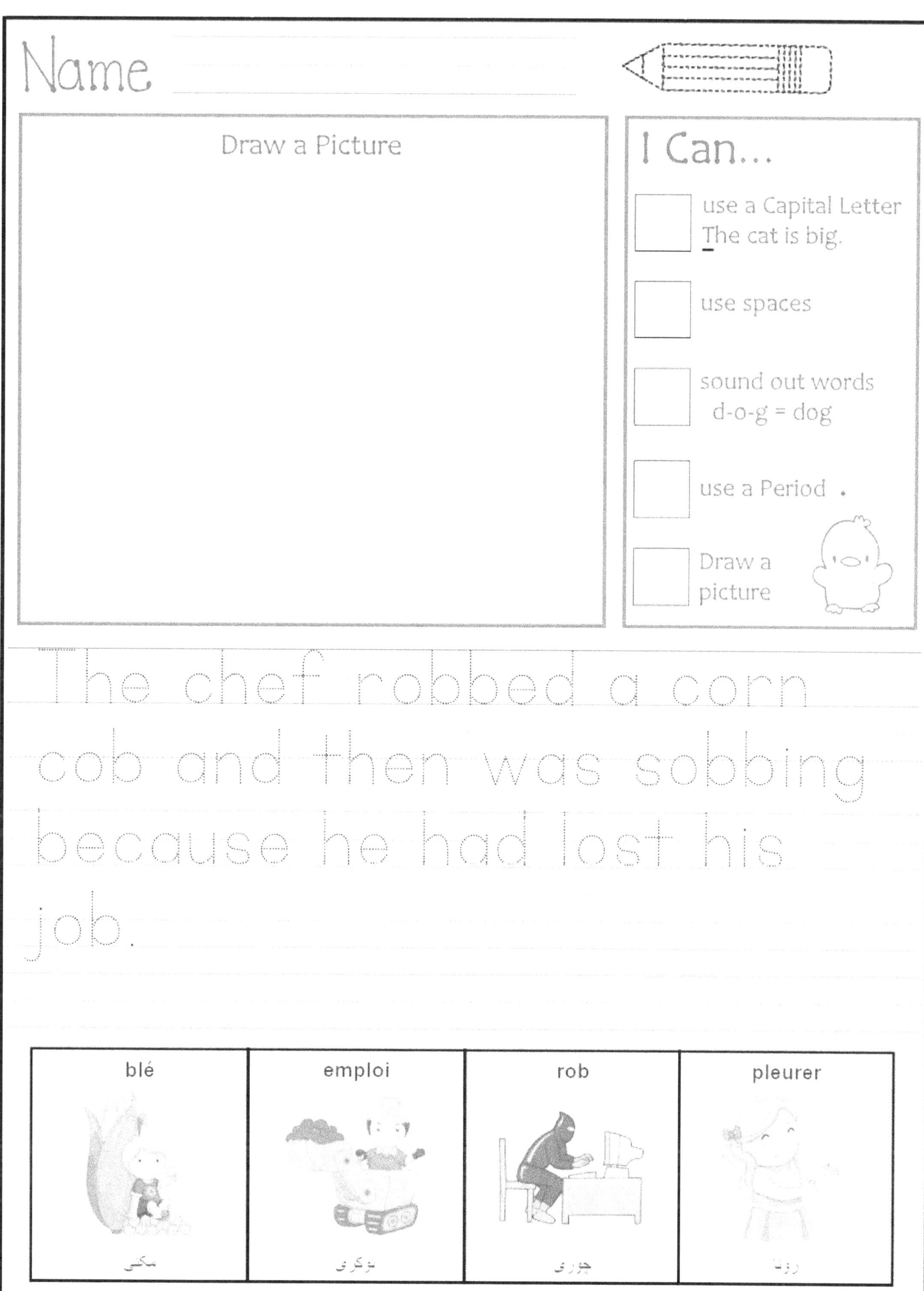

Name _______________________

Draw a Picture

I Can...

- [ ] use a Capital Letter
  <u>T</u>he cat is big.

- [ ] use spaces

- [ ] sound out words
  d-o-g = dog

- [ ] use a Period .

- [ ] Draw a picture

The chef robbed a corn cob and then was sobbing because he had lost his job.

blé	emploi	rob	pleurer

Name: ____________________ Date: ____________________

Today is: Monday Tuesday Wednesday Thursday Friday

Direction: Trace and read the sentences.

chien	porc	le jogging	bois
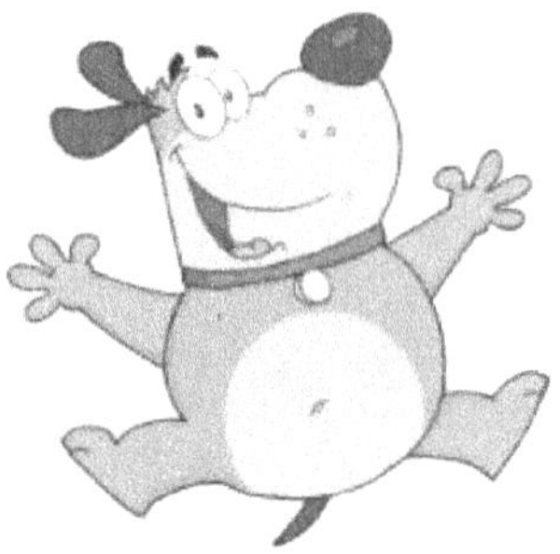	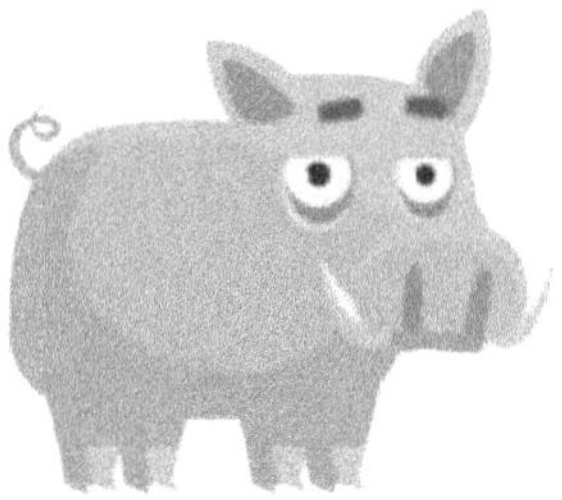	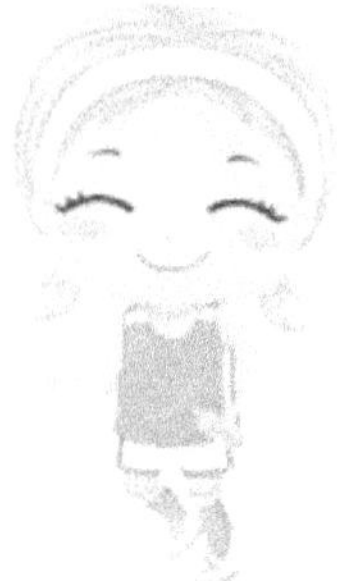	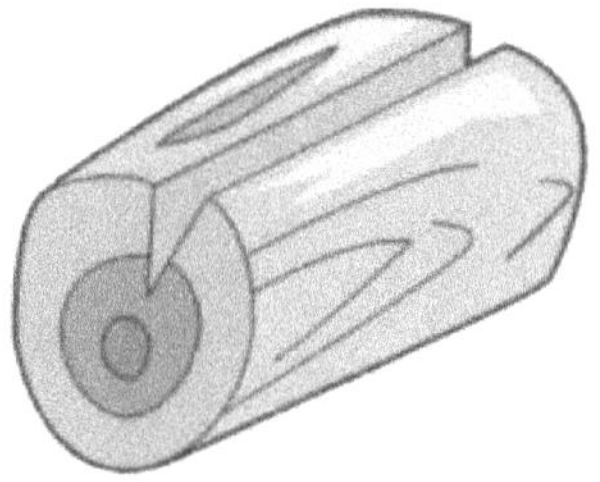
کتا	باگ	ٹہلنا	لکڑی

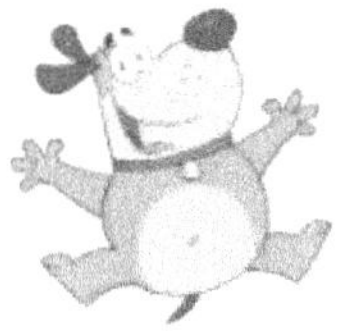 The dog is thrilled.

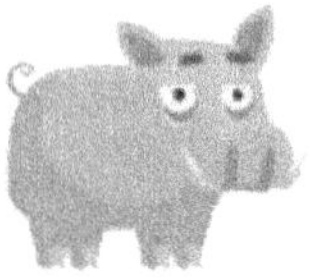 The hog is big.

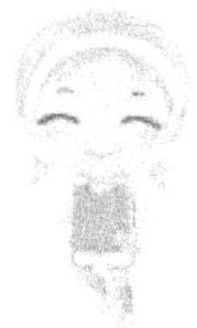 She is jogging.

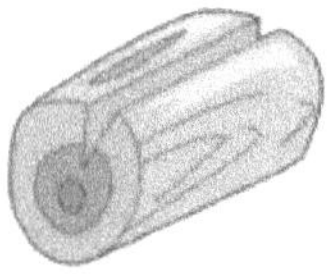 The log is small.

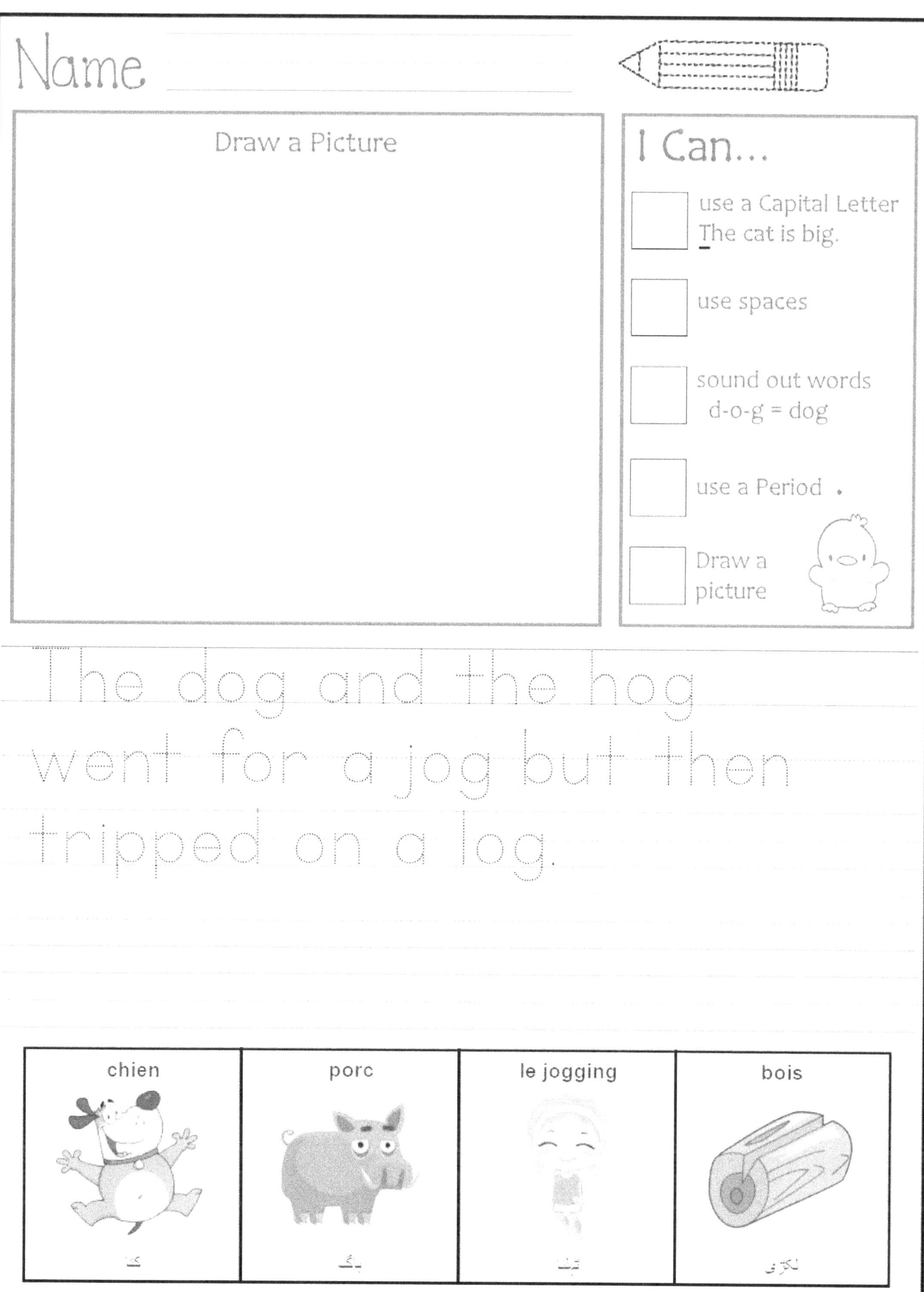

Name
Draw a Picture
I Can...
use a Capital Letter
The cat is big.
use spaces
sound out words
d-o-g = dog
use a Period .
Draw a picture
The dog and the hog went for a jog but then tripped on a log.
chien
porc
le jogging
bois

Name: ___________________ Date: _______

Today is:

| Monday | Tuesday | Wednesday |

| Thursday | Friday |

Direction: Trace and read the sentences.

| punaise | étreinte | cruche | agresser |

The bug is colorful.

She is hugging.

The jug has milk in it.

He has a mug.

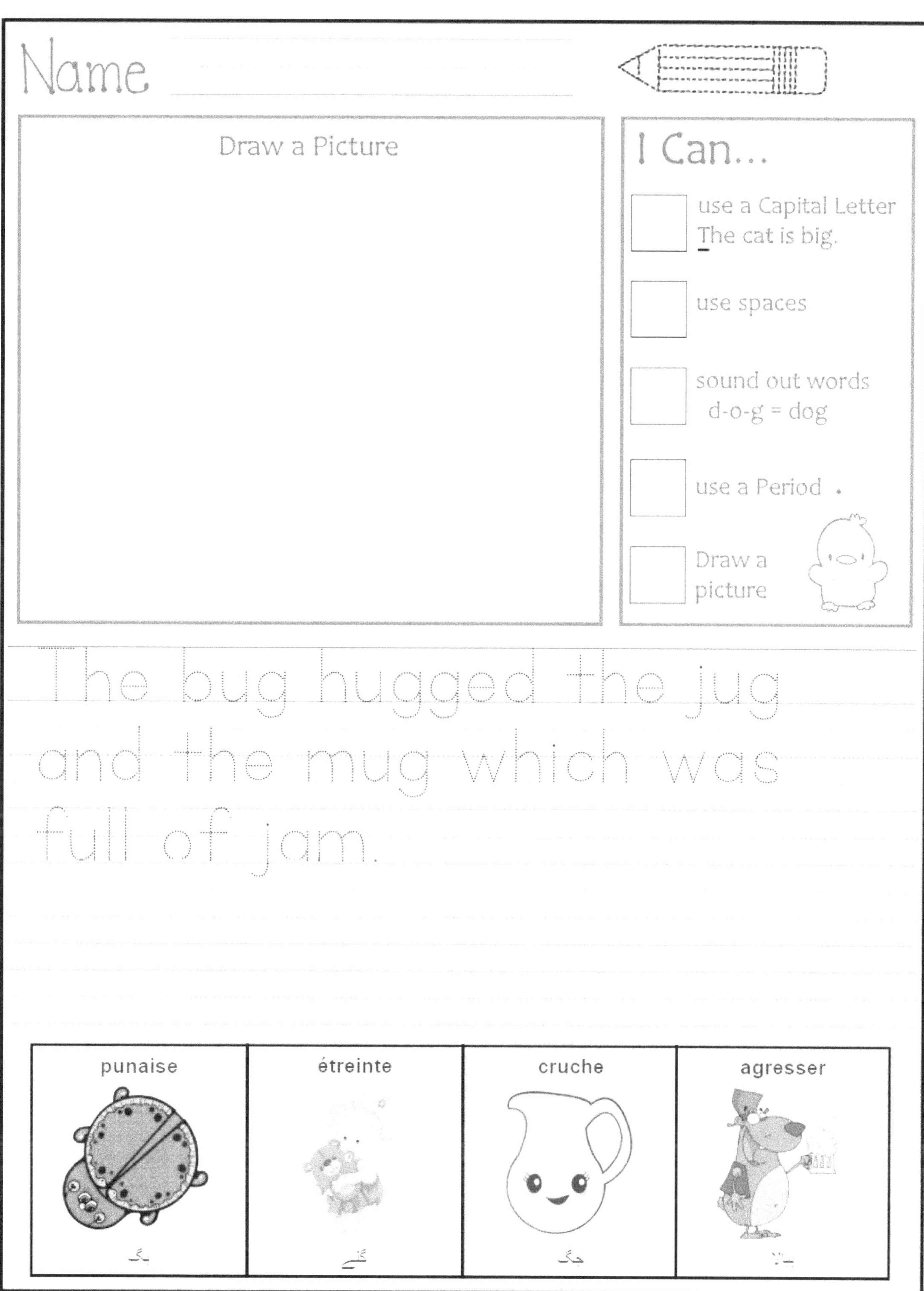

Name _______________

Draw a Picture

I Can...

- [ ] use a Capital Letter
  <u>T</u>he cat is big.

- [ ] use spaces

- [ ] sound out words
  d-o-g = dog

- [ ] use a Period .

- [ ] Draw a picture

The bug hugged the jug
and the mug which was
full of jam.

punaise	étreinte	cruche	agresser

Name: ____________________ Date: ____________________

Today is: Monday | Tuesday | Wednesday | Thursday | Friday

Direction: Trace and read the sentences.

lit	point	chaud	pot
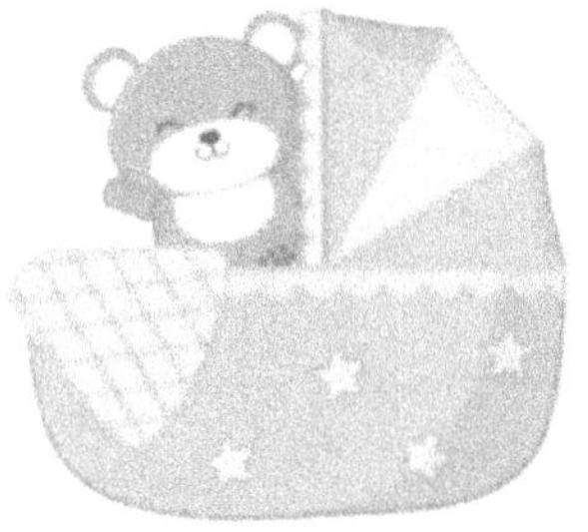	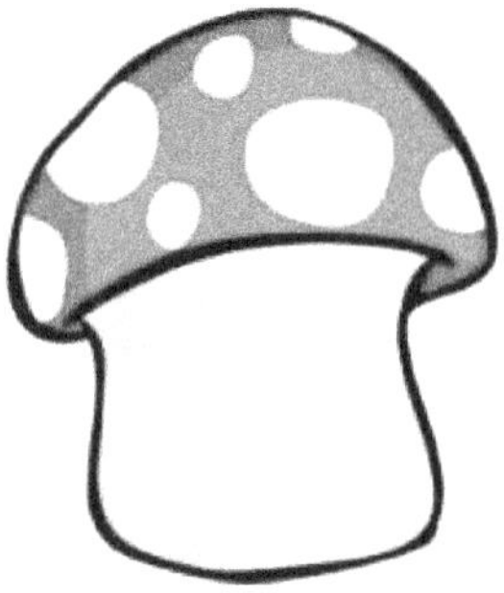	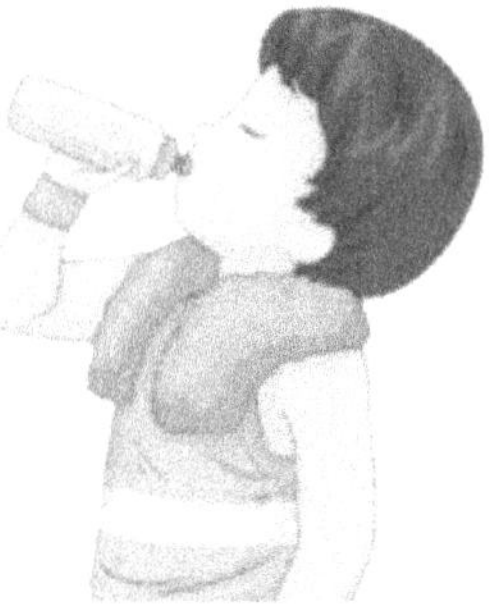	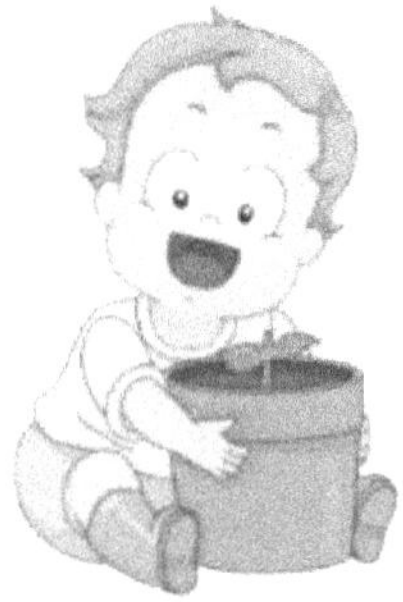
بستر	ڈاٹ	گرم	برتن

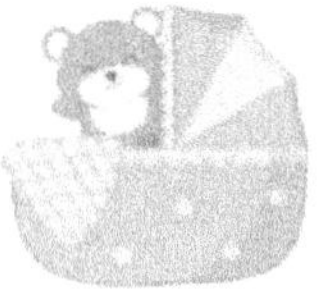 This is my cot.

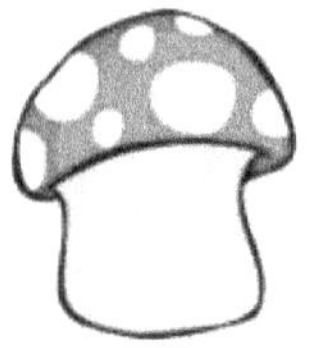 There are many dots.

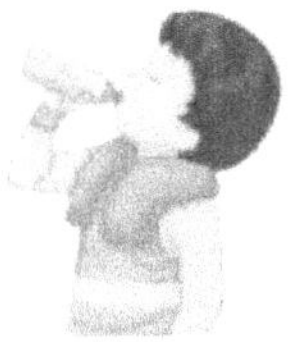 It is very hot.

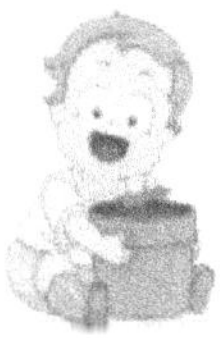 He has a plant pot.

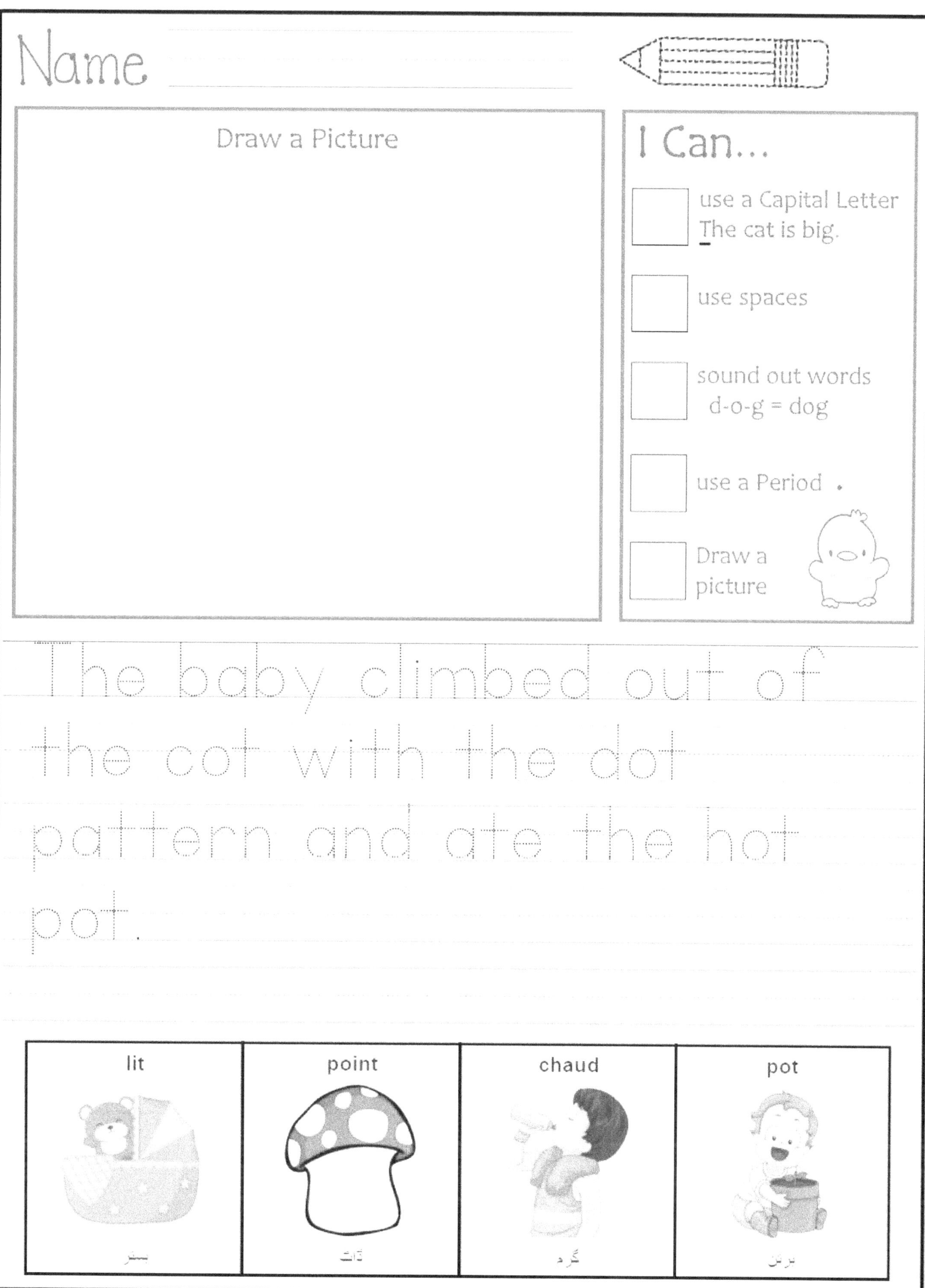

Name

Draw a Picture

I Can...

use a Capital Letter
The cat is big.

use spaces

sound out words
d-o-g = dog

use a Period .

Draw a
picture

The baby climbed out of
the cot with the dot
pattern and ate the hot
pot.

lit
point
chaud
pot

Name: _______________   Date: _______________

Today is: | Monday | Tuesday | Wednesday |
           | Thursday | Friday |

Direction: Read the words and make a sentence.

amusement	pistolet	courir	soleil
مزه	بندوق	رن	شورج

Name ___________________________

Draw a Picture

I Can...

- [ ] use a Capital Letter
  The cat is big.

- [ ] use spaces

- [ ] sound out words
  d-o-g = dog

- [ ] use a Period .

- [ ] Draw a picture

Name: ___________________   Date: ___________________

Today is: | Monday | Tuesday | Wednesday |
           | Thursday | Friday |

Name: _______________________   Date: _______________

Today is: | Monday | Tuesday | Wednesday |
| Thursday | Friday |

Direction: Read the words and make a sentence.

sac	chiffon	étiquette	remuer
سَگ	جِھِیڑا	تیگ	واگ

Name

Draw a Picture

I Can...

☐ use a Capital Letter
The cat is big.

☐ use spaces

☐ sound out words
d-o-g = dog

☐ use a Period .

☐ Draw a picture

Name: ___________________   Date: ___________

Today is:

Name: ___________________ Date: ___________

Today is: | Monday | Tuesday | Wednesday |
| Thursday | Friday |

Direction: Read the words and make a sentence.

canettes	homme	la poêle	van

Name

I Can...

- [ ] use a Capital Letter
  The cat is big.
- [ ] use spaces
- [ ] sound out words
  d-o-g = dog
- [ ] use a Period .
- [ ] Draw a picture

Name: _______________   Date: _______________

Today is: [Monday] [Tuesday] [Wednesday]
[Thursday] [Friday]

Name: __________________ Date: __________

Today is:

Monday   Tuesday   Wednesday   Thursday   Friday

Direction: Read the words and make a sentence.

couper	intestin	cabane	écrou

Name

Draw a Picture

I Can...

use a Capital Letter
The cat is big.

use spaces

sound out words
d-o-g = dog

use a Period .

Draw a
picture

Name: Date:

Today is: Monday Tuesday Wednesday
Thursday Friday

Name: _______________ Date: _______________

Today is: Monday Tuesday Wednesday

Thursday Friday

Direction: Read the words and make a sentence.

graisse	chat	chapeau	tapis
جربی	کِت	ثوبی	چتائی

Name ___________________________

Draw a Picture

I Can...

- [ ] use a Capital Letter
  <u>T</u>he cat is big.

- [ ] use spaces

- [ ] sound out words
  d-o-g = dog

- [ ] use a Period .

- [ ] Draw a picture

Name: _______________   Date: _______________

Today is: Monday Tuesday Wednesday
          Thursday Friday

Name: _______________________ Date: _______________

Today is: Monday   Tuesday   Wednesday

Thursday   Friday

Direction: Read the words and make a sentence.

taxi	laboratoire	languette	crabe
TAXI			
تیکسی	لیب	تہ	ککڑے

Draw a Picture

I Can...

- use a Capital Letter
  The cat is big.

- use spaces

- sound out words
  d-o-g = dog

- use a Period .

- Draw a picture

Name: _______________ Date: _______________

Today is: [Monday] [Tuesday] [Wednesday]
[Thursday] [Friday]

Name: _______________________ Date: _______________

Today is: Monday   Tuesday   Wednesday

Thursday   Friday

Direction: Read the words and make a sentence.

jambon	confiture	mouton	palourde
بَام	حَم	بهيزة	مُیْل

Name _______________________

<table>
<tr><td>

Draw a Picture

</td><td>

I Can...

☐ use a Capital Letter
The cat is big.

☐ use spaces

☐ sound out words
d-o-g = dog

☐ use a Period .

☐ Draw a
picture

</td></tr>
</table>

Name: _______________   Date: _______________

Today is:

| Monday | Tuesday | Wednesday |

| Thursday | Friday |

Name: _______________________ Date: _______________

Today is: | Monday | | Tuesday | | Wednesday |

| Thursday | | Friday |

Direction: Read the words and make a sentence.

| lit | de premier plan | rouge | mariage |

Name

Draw a Picture

I Can...

- [ ] use a Capital Letter
  The cat is big.

- [ ] use spaces

- [ ] sound out words
  d-o-g = dog

- [ ] use a Period .

- [ ] Draw a picture

Name: Date:

Today is: Monday   Tuesday   Wednesday

Thursday   Friday

Name: ___________________   Date: ___________

Today is: | Monday | Tuesday | Wednesday |
| Thursday | Friday |

Direction: Read the words and make a sentence.

mauvais	papa	furieux	triste
برا	والد	بیگن	اداس

Name ______________________

<table>
<tr><td>Draw a Picture</td><td>I Can...</td></tr>
</table>

Draw a Picture

I Can...

- [ ] use a Capital Letter
  The cat is big.

- [ ] use spaces

- [ ] sound out words
  d-o-g = dog

- [ ] use a Period .

- [ ] Draw a picture

Name: _______________ Date: _______________

Today is: Monday Tuesday Wednesday

Thursday Friday

Name: ___________________ Date: ___________

Today is: [Monday] [Tuesday] [Wednesday]
           [Thursday] [Friday]

Direction: Read the words and make a sentence.

animal den	poule	écuries	dix
بيات	بيت دجاج	اصطبل	عشرة

Name

Draw a Picture

I Can...

☐ use a Capital Letter
The cat is big.

☐ use spaces

☐ sound out words
d-o-g = dog

☐ use a Period .

☐ Draw a picture

Name:
Date:
Today is:
Monday
Tuesday
Wednesday
Thursday
Friday

Name: _________________________ Date: _______________

Today is: Monday Tuesday Wednesday Thursday Friday

Direction: Read the words and make a sentence.

gommeux	maman	somme	tambour
جبجيا	مال	رقم	دّهول

Name _______________________

Draw a Picture

I Can...

- [ ] use a Capital Letter
The cat is big.

- [ ] use spaces

- [ ] sound out words
d-o-g = dog

- [ ] use a Period .

- [ ] Draw a picture

Name: _______________   Date: _______________

Today is:

| Monday | Tuesday | Wednesday |

| Thursday | Friday |

offre	cacher	enfant	couvercle

Draw a Picture

I Can...

- [ ] use a Capital Letter
  The cat is big.

- [ ] use spaces

- [ ] sound out words
  d-o-g = dog

- [ ] use a Period .

- [ ] Draw a picture

Name: Date:

Today is:

Name: _______________________ Date: _______________

Today is: Monday Tuesday Wednesday Thursday Friday

Direction: Read the words and make a sentence.

gros	creuser	porc	perruque
بڑا	کھودنا	سور	وگ

Name ___________________

Draw a Picture

I Can...

- [ ] use a Capital Letter
  <u>T</u>he cat is big.

- [ ] use spaces

- [ ] sound out words
  d-o-g = dog

- [ ] use a Period .

- [ ] Draw a picture

Name: _______________   Date: _______________

Today is: Monday | Tuesday | Wednesday
Thursday | Friday

Name: _______________________   Date: _______________

Today is: | Monday | Tuesday | Wednesday |
| Thursday | Friday |

Direction: Read the words and make a sentence.

| poubelle | ailette | épingle | gagner |

Name _______________________

Draw a Picture

I Can...

- [ ] use a Capital Letter
  <u>T</u>he cat is big.

- [ ] use spaces

- [ ] sound out words
  d-o-g = dog

- [ ] use a Period .

- [ ] Draw a picture

Name: Date:

Today is: Monday Tuesday Wednesday Thursday Friday

Name: _______________________ Date: _______________________

Today is: Monday Tuesday Wednesday Thursday Friday

Direction: Read the words and make a sentence.

hanche	lèvres	pincer	boisson

Name

Draw a Picture

I Can...

☐ use a Capital Letter
The cat is big.

☐ use spaces

☐ sound out words
d-o-g = dog

☐ use a Period .

☐ Draw a
picture

Name: _______________________   Date: _______________________

Today is:

| Monday | Tuesday | Wednesday |

| Thursday | Friday |

Name: _______________________   Date: _______________

Today is: [Monday] [Tuesday] [Wednesday]
[Thursday] [Friday]

Direction: Read the words and make a sentence.

en forme	frappé	trousse	asseoir

Name _______________________

<table>
<tr><td>Draw a Picture</td><td>I Can...</td></tr>
</table>

Draw a Picture

I Can...

☐ use a Capital Letter
The cat is big.

☐ use spaces

☐ sound out words
d-o-g = dog

☐ use a Period .

☐ Draw a picture

Name: Date:

Today is: Monday   Tuesday   Wednesday

Thursday   Friday

Name: _______________________ Date: _______________

Today is: | Monday | Tuesday | Wednesday |
| Thursday | Friday |

Direction: Read the words and make a sentence.

blé	emploi	rob	pleurer
سکئی	نوکری	چوری	رونا

Name ___________________________

Draw a Picture

I Can...

☐ use a Capital Letter
The cat is big.

☐ use spaces

☐ sound out words
d-o-g = dog

☐ use a Period .

☐ Draw a
picture

Name: _______________   Date: _______________

Today is: Monday   Tuesday   Wednesday
          Thursday   Friday

Name: _________________________ Date: _______

Today is: | Monday | Tuesday | Wednesday |
| Thursday | Friday |

Direction: Read the words and make a sentence.

| chien | porc | le jogging | bois |

(Arabic labels under each picture)

Name _______________

Draw a Picture

I Can...

- [ ] use a Capital Letter
  The cat is big.

- [ ] use spaces

- [ ] sound out words
  d-o-g = dog

- [ ] use a Period .

- [ ] Draw a picture

Name: _______________ Date: _______________

Today is: Monday   Tuesday   Wednesday
            Thursday   Friday

Name: ___________________ Date: ___________

Today is:

[Monday] [Tuesday] [Wednesday]
[Thursday] [Friday]

Direction: Read the words and make a sentence.

punaise	étreinte	cruche	agresser
بگ	گلے	جگ	پیلا

Name ________________________________

<table>
<tr><td>Draw a Picture</td><td>I Can...</td></tr>
</table>

Draw a Picture

I Can...

☐ use a Capital Letter
The cat is big.

☐ use spaces

☐ sound out words
d-o-g = dog

☐ use a Period .

☐ Draw a
picture

Name: _______________   Date: _______________

Today is: [Monday] [Tuesday] [Wednesday]
[Thursday] [Friday]

Name: _______________________ Date: _______________

Today is: [Monday] [Tuesday] [Wednesday]
[Thursday] [Friday]

Direction: Read the words and make a sentence.

lit	point	chaud	pot
بستر	ٹاک	گرم	برتن

Name ____________________

Draw a Picture

I Can...

- [ ] use a Capital Letter
  The cat is big.

- [ ] use spaces

- [ ] sound out words
  d-o-g = dog

- [ ] use a Period .

- [ ] Draw a picture

Name: Date:

Today is: Monday   Tuesday   Wednesday

          Thursday   Friday